SUR VIV ING CULTURE

When Character and Your World Collide

BY EDWARD E. MOODY

randall house

114 Bush Rd I Nashville, TN 37217
randallhouse.com

dedication

For Mackenzie and Mitchell:
May God use you to point our culture toward Him.

table of contents

Introduction

This is a tough time to be a teen. Maybe you feel like you are all alone as you try to follow the Lord. Perhaps your peers make fun of you and your lifestyle. You are not alone. I see a lot of teens. As a pastor, I see them during the week when they've been at school and on the weekends I see them as they interact with peers. Sometimes they feel very lonely. I also see a lot of college students in my work as a college professor. I watch them as they prepare to go into some difficult environments and try to help others. Many of them are Christians striving to remain firm in their faith. Can you stay true to your faith and succeed in a corrupt culture? Yes, you can, if you walk with the LORD.

In this book I hope you will see that if you are a believer, you never walk alone. You have a God who has made you to survive and thrive in this culture, and if you will follow Him He will bring you through. He will also use you in ways you never imagined to influence this culture.

I know. I've seen it. I've experienced it. Long ago I was a young person just like you, trying to serve God and do what I could to help others. Often it seemed like I was alone, and would have no impact upon the culture I was trying to help. I learned God was always at work and I simply needed to be prepared to serve and He would create the opportunities. For example, after I finished my training to be a professional counselor it was time for me to begin my clinical training. I chose a place where I thought I could make a difference. Just before

I began my internship, I met with the director of the facility. After a good meeting he noted, "I see you have a religious background, you know you can't talk about that here." I left feeling a little dejected, as if I might not be able to contribute. After all, it was my faith that energized me to try to help people. The next Monday when I arrived to begin my internship many of the staff members met me in the facility parking lot. They informed me that a staff member had been killed in an accident over the weekend and the whole facility was in turmoil. The director asked to see me. I went into his office and he recapped what had transpired over the weekend. Then he noted, "I see you have this religious background, I wonder if you could have some kind of meeting with all of the youth, kind of a chapel and help our folks deal with this death." I thought, yes, I can help with that. My faith was valuable to them after all. Throughout my life I've had many similar experiences. I've learned that it is important to be ready. I believe God made me to help with moments like this. I believe God made you to use you in His work. This book is for you, to help you see that God made you capable of surviving culture in the midst of corruption and that He will use you at some point to help those around you.

Chapter 1

Be Ready

You have probably heard all the negative statistics. Fewer than 18 percent of 18 to 29 year-olds attend church today. The number of atheists and agnostics are on the rise. One-third of the people under the age of 30 characterize themselves as believing nothing in particular.[1] It sounds like our situation is pretty bleak and that most people will be skeptical if not outright antagonistic toward Christianity in the future. If this data is correct, the only Christianity the world will see in the future will be from their classmate, co-worker, or neighbor. Some will succumb to the influence of the culture and fall away from Christianity. Others, though faithful, will be ineffective as they cocoon themselves away from the world. Rather than being discouraged, I hope you will see this as an opportunity. God is not surprised by any of this. In fact, He has been preparing you for just this kind of thing all of your life. By the way, He has dealt with all of this before.

Ecclesiastes 1:9 tells us, "What has been is what will be, and what has been done is what will be done, and there is nothing new under the sun." In many ways, the world you live in has changed and is unlike that of your parents and grandparents. In other ways, nothing has really changed. There is nothing new under the sun. That means you have an opportunity to learn from those from the past.

Brothers from Another Era

Some 2,600 years ago, God used four young men named Daniel, Hananiah, Mishael, and Azariah to impact their culture. Their situation was not unlike ours in many ways. There was a god on every corner, perhaps a temple on each block. Similarly, our pluralistic society seems to believe in any and everything. Yet, they went about their day without the grumbling and disputing that characterizes many of us. Instead of succumbing to negative influence, they held fast showing strong character. Instead of harming, they were helpful, providing light to those around them. Instead of becoming like the world in which they lived, God worked through them to point those they encountered to Him. If we wish to influence our culture, we will need to study their story.

Any time someone provides an example to follow, we have a tendency to say, "Yes, but." If someone gives you a model for living godly in your school or workplace, the tendency is to think, "Sure, but he didn't have to deal with my peers or my teachers." So, let us get some context for what these four endured.

In 605 B.C., terror descended upon Judah as an invading army poured into Jerusalem. The economy collapsed, the government was disbanded, and entire neighborhoods disappeared. These four found themselves in the middle of these horrific events. They were seized and taken to Babylon. (Check out 2 Kings 24 for the entire tale.)

The events these four endured were worse than the Great Depression, the attack upon Pearl Harbor, and the September 11, 2001 attacks combined. After all of this, they found themselves in the middle of a corrupt culture being bombarded with its messages.

So why do we need to study their story? Because they endured the worst, some of the most horrific scenarios our brains could conjure. How did they respond? How did they live in a culture so against the truth of God? Their example can encourage, instruct, and challenge us as difficult encounters arise in our lives. If they brought God's message in the most hostile situations, then how can we present Christ to our friends, family, and those with whom we interact regularly?

Know God, Know Yourself

The Bible says in Ephesians 6:10-11, 13: "Finally, be strong in the Lord and in the strength of his might. Put on the whole armor of God, that you may be able to stand against the schemes of the devil. Therefore take up the whole armor of God, that you may be able to withstand in the evil day, and having done all, to stand firm." I suspect Daniel, Hananiah, Mishael, and Azariah knew the Lord and had put on the whole armor of God before they were taken from Judah. To survive and thrive in your culture, you too need to place your faith in the Lord and derive your strength from Him by putting on the armor of God, using the tools only He can give you to prepare you to survive. It is tempting to rush into the corrupt culture and do what you can to have a positive influence upon it. However, this is not advisable. You must be properly prepared or such good intentions could lead to tragic consequences. Entering the culture unprepared is akin to a well-meaning firefighter entering a burning building without the proper equipment. If you are not prepared, you will become a victim of the corrupt culture.

Proper preparation means that you know God and you know yourself. What are your strengths? What are your weaknesses? What are your vulnerabilities? Ask yourself: Who am I? What am I? What is really important to me?

Who are you when you are Judean, and Judah lies in ruins? Who are you when you are Christian, and your culture cheapens Him? What are you to do when the kingdom you have spent your life preparing to serve has been conquered? What are you to do when the culture attacks what is important to you?

Daniel, Hananiah, Mishael, and Azariah found themselves serving in the kingdom that destroyed their homeland, and perhaps killed many they loved. When they entered Babylon, they found themselves in a land unlike anything they had seen. The Babylonians were experts in magic devoted to other gods.

Daniel and his friends were immersed into this culture. They found themselves in classrooms studying polytheistic literature where magic, sorcery, charms, and astrology were valued.

They were unlike many of the young people who accompanied them and began taking on the ways of Babylon. Perhaps many of their peers left behind their "outdated and obsolete" faith.

Yet, these young men were secure enough in their relationship with God and their knowledge of God to be able to study this material without it undermining their faith. Their previous time with God and study of Scripture had prepared them to withstand this onslaught of false teaching. They knew God and therefore were undeterred. Similarly, you may find yourself bombarded with evolution, polytheism, and moral relativism where wrong is portrayed as right and right as wrong; so you too must be certain of your relationship with God, and what you believe.

When you are in the culture, be in the habit of asking yourself, "Who is influencing whom?" Am I influencing those around me toward God or are they drawing me away from God.

When you are in a situation where you are in over your head, you find yourself getting confused, or encountering severe temptation, get help and at times it may be necessary, at least temporarily, to get out of a situation. For example, if you find yourself getting confused when you are with a certain friend, you might need to withdraw from them until you are more certain of what you believe and better prepared to deal for a time with the challenges they present.

Names with a Purpose

Along with knowing the God they worshipped and how He crafted and designed their identity, these Hebrew men carried names with a purpose. Daniel means, "God is my judge." When he heard his name, Daniel was reminded that God was watching over him no matter how unjust the world may have seemed.

Hananiah means, "God has been gracious." When he heard his name, Hananiah was reminded that God was good to him regardless of the circumstances he endured.

Mishael means, "Who is what God is?" When he heard his name, Mishael was reminded of the power of God as he faced a polytheistic environment. There may have been a god on every corner (or at every gate around the city), but there was no god like Jehovah.

Azariah means, "God is my help." He was reminded of the help that can come only from God as he encountered numerous crises. The naming of these four implies they had received strong spiritual preparation in their younger days. Yet, no matter if you have enjoyed a healthy upbringing with parents immersed in and following God's Word or experienced the complete opposite or anything in between, if you are God's, then He has His seal upon you. The names of these four indicate they belonged to Jehovah, the God of Judah just as you do. Ephesians 4:30 tells us "And do not grieve the Holy Spirit of God, by whom you were sealed for the day of redemption." You belong to God, but that does not mean the culture will not try to change you just as they tried to change Daniel, Hananiah, Mishael, and Azariah by changing their names as you will see shortly. You are His, and everything that comes with it. No culture, no pressure, no scientific data, can alter that distinction. With that basis, confidence, hope, and faith grow strong.

A Challenge Emerges

When you are part of a corrupt culture, the forces of that culture will try to change you. In the Bible, Babylon always refers to a corrupt culture. Interestingly, Daniel writes they were taken to the land of Shinar (Daniel 1:2), where there was an immediate assault upon their identity that came in the form of a name change.

Daniel's name was changed to Belteshazzar, which meant, "May a god protect his life" or "A goddess protect the king." Hananiah's name was changed to Shadrach that may invoke the name of the Babylonian god Marduk. Mishael's name was changed to Meshach and the meaning of this name is less certain. Azariah's name was changed to Abednego, which may mean "Servant of (the god) Nabu."[2] The king was probably immersing the youth in the customs of the Chaldeans so that Judah might become a distant memory.

An Attack on Your Name

Similarly, you will experience attacks on your identity like, "Jesus was just a man," and "The Bible is a manmade book." You may even see your faith described as something you do not recognize. Daniel, Hananiah, Mishael, and Azariah were undeterred when the Babylonians changed their names. You too want to be undeterred by attacks upon your faith. For this to occur you must be immersed in the Word of God and have a deep relationship with God.

The Bible, Your New Best Friend

Daniel and his buddies did not become scholars of the Torah overnight. They most likely studied it from early childhood. When you become a follower of Christ, the Holy Spirit does not magically endow you with the ability to write a commentary on Revelation. God did not design spiritual growth that way.

We do not grow physically without a steady diet. The tendency is to eat at least three times a day. When we miss a meal, we deal with hunger pangs and lack of energy and have other ailments. In addition, eating a balanced diet is important. Though we might think a diet of chips and soda would be wonderful, we know that eventually it will have a negative impact upon us. If there is anything missing from our diet, we do not operate at our optimal level physically and we are more susceptible to disease.

Just like strong muscles or healthy bones are not developed by a hit-and-miss diet or a big binge on veggies, spiritual growth is derived from a steady diet in the Bible. Regular study of God's Word to us comes in a variety of ways: personal study, small group study, Christian education/Sunday School courses, and listening to sermons, just to name the most common. These types of activities create a healthy, balanced diet of time in the Scripture.

To benefit from the Bible, gather the tools you will need just as you gather utensils before a meal. Get a Bible in a translation you understand and a Bible dictionary or handbook that will help you get some context for what you are reading. I like the ESV study Bible. It is a good idea to compare passages in different translations at the Biblegateway.com website or with the Biblegateway or YouVersion apps. Use a journal or notebook to record your observations, what you learn about God, and what you need to apply to your life. This allows you to process the Word just as the body processes food.

Ask God to direct you as you study the Bible and to help you apply it to your life.

It helps if you are able to have routine times and places where you read the Bible and pray so that it becomes a habit in your life. Jesus often had His quiet time during the morning hours (Mark 1:35), but there are no strict guidelines about how. We are simply instructed to search the Scriptures daily (Deuteronomy 17:19; Acts 17:11). If you struggle with where to start, begin with the book of John. Read a chapter from Proverbs each day. (On the first of the month, read the first chapter and so forth.) Or read and pray a psalm each day. Or read a chapter from the Old Testament and another from the New Testament. Do not get too bogged down in the what, but make sure you have a daily time that you spend with God. Focus more on the Who and growing closer to Him!

When you read a portion of Scripture, consider these questions:
- What did this passage mean to the original hearers?
- What is the timeless principle?

- What does it teach me about God?
- Based on this passage, how can I apply it?

Why does this matter? People who are in top physical shape are more likely to survive an injury or sudden illness. Their bodies draw upon the strength they have developed when injured. Similarly, when faced with a spiritual crisis, you must draw upon the strength you have developed over time and your relationship with the Lord if you are to endure. Daniel, Hananiah, Mishael, and Azariah knew their God well long before the Babylonians tried to change their names. Similarly, you cannot wait until you find yourself in situations where you are the only Christian around and people are trying to change you to develop your relationship with God.

In all circumstances take up the shield of faith, with which you can extinguish all the flaming darts of the evil one; and take the helmet of salvation, and the sword of the Spirit, which is the word of God.
Ephesians 6:16-17

Application of the Word

You will see later that the faith of Daniel, Hananiah, Mishael, and Azariah as well as their application of the Word of God helped them deal with multiple attacks (or flaming darts of the evil one). Application of the Word of God is to spiritual growth as exercise is to physical growth. Unused biblical knowledge is similar to unused muscles. Without use deterioration results.

Constant reading and thinking about the Scripture will change you and how you deal with various problems.

For example, Dr. Dan Ariely conducted some research indicating that cheating is prevalent on college campuses. He found one situation where people were less likely to cheat. One group of students was asked to recall the Ten Commandments before taking a test.[3] Most of these students did not know the Ten Commandments and none could recall all of them. However, taking the time to recall them and consider some of them significantly reduced cheating. This demonstrates that taking the time to think about the Word of God can help you stay on track. Imagine the results that could be achieved for a person motivated to obey the Word.

With each step you take applying the Bible to your life, you are strengthening yourself for the challenges you will face in the future. You should also find that your relationship with the Lord grows deeper. Applying the Word, leads to the Word abiding in you and an intimate knowledge of it and the Lord. As an example, consider Psalm 46. If Daniel, Hananiah, Mishael, and Azariah knew this passage, how might they have applied it? How might you apply it in your own life?

The Worst Case Scenario Psalm
Psalm 46

God is our refuge and strength, a very present help in trouble. Therefore we will not fear though the earth gives way, though the mountains be moved into the heart of the sea, though its waters roar and foam, though the mountains tremble at its swelling. Selah (emphasis mine).

What did this passage mean to the original hearers? It meant that God was with them as they were encountering great difficulty and He would help them. The mountains falling into the middle of the sea would be the most traumatic event one could imagine (e.g., like the overthrow of your nation or the death of a parent). Instead of fear, the reader is instructed to concentrate upon God's ability to help them in any situation, even one as desperate as the mountains falling into the sea.

What is the timeless principle? God provides refuge and strength for us at the worst times of our lives.

What do I learn about God? He will be my refuge, my strength in the most difficult moments of my life.

What do I need to do based upon this passage? Ask yourself, "What are the worst events that could transpire in my life?" Think about how God would help you and give you strength during these. God will be with you when your world is turned upside down and when your life is calm. God is our refuge, our help, every day all the time. You do not know what the future holds, but you can know that God will help you, especially at the most difficult time of a crisis.

Have a period daily where you pause and reflect upon God. It is this kind of work that will help you as you encounter various difficulties in your life. As you look at Scripture like this, consider how the same God who helped Jacob, Daniel, Hananiah, Mishael, and Azariah will help you.

I like reading *The Complete Worst-Case Scenario Survival Handbook.* There is an entry about how to escape from a giant octopus, and a charging rhino. Then there are more serious entries like surviving if your parachute does not open, and evading a stampede of shoppers. Some are pretty silly but others are fairly serious like surviving a rollover in a car, or how to perform a tracheotomy.

While we truly have no idea what the future holds in terms of personal triumphs and tragedies (giant octopi or not) or in terms of the evolution of our culture, God does know. He is preparing us today for what we will face tomorrow.

God knew what would happen to Daniel, Hananiah, Mishael, and Azariah. Isaiah 39:7 says, "And some of your own sons, who will come from you, whom you will father, shall be taken away, and they shall be eunuchs in the palace of the king of Babylon." This verse was written between 750 and 690 B.C., yet Isaiah prophesied about the events of 605 B.C. during Daniel, Hananiah, Mishael, and Azariah's life.

God also knows what is coming your way. In addition to studying the Bible, it is important that you become capable of defending it.

Incidentally, the book of Daniel is one of the favorite targets of critics. Many deny that Daniel was a prophet because in Hebrew Bibles Daniel is located in the Writings section.

Some claim that someone other than Daniel wrote the book of Daniel, and that Daniel was not written until the second century B.C.

As an example of how to address these issues, consider a brief defense of the book of Daniel. The book of Daniel was likely located in the Writings section of the Hebrew Bible because Daniel's ministry was to the heathen court rather than the people of Israel.

By reading the New Testament, one will clearly see that Jesus viewed Daniel as a prophet, and his book as truth. Matthew 24:15 says, "So when you see the abomination of desolation spoken by the prophet Daniel, standing in the holy place (let the reader understand)."

Ezekiel, a contemporary of Daniel, wrote highly of him: "Even if these three men, Noah, Daniel, and Job, were in it, they would deliver but their own lives by their righteousness, declares the Lord GOD. Even if Noah, Daniel, and Job were in it, as I live, declares the Lord GOD, they would deliver neither son nor daughter. They would deliver but their own lives by their righteousness (Ezekiel 14:14, 20).

Some have claimed that Ezekiel was referring to a different Daniel but consider Ezekiel 28:3, "You are indeed wiser than Daniel; no secret is hidden from you." Ezekiel's Daniel sounds like the one in the book that bears his name.

Sometimes you will need to utilize other valuable resources to defend Scripture. For example, in *Daniel: Tyndale Old Testament Commentary* by J. G. Baldwin, you learn that the book of Daniel refers to people and events that would not otherwise be known from biblical events or history.[4]

Other commentators indicate there is nothing in the original Hebrew and Aramaic language of the book that precludes an authorship of the sixth century B.C.[5]

When you find you need to learn more about a particular book of the Bible, you can utilize commentaries. Many of these can be found in libraries; however, not all will be helpful. Look for commentaries by those who believe the Bible is the inspired Word of God. There are two books that rank commentaries according to reliability: *Old Testament Commentary Survey* by T. Longman and *New Testament Commentary Survey* by D. A. Carson.

Critics like to attack the biblical account of creation and the historical accuracy of the Bible so it helps to be familiar with work that addresses these attacks. Here is a list of resources where you can find podcasts that will help prepare you for these issues.

Podcast Resources
See also SurvivingCulture.com

Title	Description	Website
Answers . . . with Ken Ham	Daily podcast about Creation	www.answersingenesis.org
Apologetics 315 Interviews	315 interviews of Christian apologists	www.apologetics315.com
Coffee Cup Apologetics	Brief enough to have apologetics over lunch	www.ccapologetics.wordpress.com
Defenders Podcast	Dr. William Lane Craig's Sunday school class on Christian doctrine and apologetics	www.reasonablefaith.org
The Voice of Truth	4 minute apologetic updates from Dr. Norman Geisler	www.normangeisler.net
Josh McDowell Ministry	Weekly messages from Josh McDowell	www.joshradio.org
Lee Strobel	Find answers to your faith questions	www.leestrobel.com

Title	Description	Website
Ravi Zacharias International Ministries	Helping the thinkers believe; helping the believers to think	www.rzim.org

In addition, you can find many books that address these questions.

Helpful Books

Ken Ham, *The New Answers in Genesis Boxed Set (Vol. 1-3)*—A close look at questions about evolution.

C. S. Lewis, *The C. S. Lewis Signature Classics*—Includes *Mere Christianity, The Screwtape Letters, The Problem of Pain*

Josh McDowell, *The New Evidence That Demands a Verdict*—Two bestselling volumes in one, a classic defense of the faith.

Josh McDowell and Sean McDowell, *More Than a Carpenter*—Finding real answers in Jesus Christ.

Josh McDowell and Dave Sterrett, *Is the Bible True . . . Really? A Dialogue on Skepticism, Evidence and Truth*—Questions about the truthfulness of the Bible answered from the standpoint of a college freshman in a state university.

Lee Strobel, *The Case for Christ*—A former atheistic journalist examines the history of the Christian faith.

Lee Strobel, *The Case for a Creator*—A former atheistic journalist examines evidence for a Creator.

Lee Strobel, *The Case for Faith*—A former atheistic journalist examines some of the tough questions often asked of the Christian faith.

Ravi Zacharias, *Beyond Opinion: Living the Faith We Defend*—How to defend your faith and be transformed by it.

Ravi Zacharias, *Jesus Among Other Gods*—Examines the unique truth of the Christian message and exposes the futility of other religions.

It is important to remember that not every accusation, sin, or heresy needs to be addressed by you. However, you can expect at one time or another—and likely many times—in your life, you will need to provide a defense for what you believe, what God teaches about Himself and His relationship to the world.

Instead of dodging questions about evolution and so forth, you should be confident and competent enough to look forward to opportunities to address these issues. By the way, when you do get those opportunities be clear, concise, calm, and congenial. Also, consider if you are dealing with a seeker or a scoffer.

A Diet Change

In addition to rhetoric, the Babylonians placed Daniel and his friends in challenging situations. As part of the training program, the Babylonians presented the youth with Babylonian food. For many this may not seem like a problem, but there is more going on under the surface.

Think about how food is integrally intertwined with culture. Consider the authentic food found in places like Chinatown in cities like San Francisco and New York or barbeque from North Carolina or Kansas City. We tend to talk about food when we speak of going home, and consider traditional dishes "comfort food."

This Babylonian food may have been a kind of gift, and a gift is not always a gift. Psychologist Robert Cialdini wrote about how people are influenced. He notes that we are likely to comply with requests from others after receiving an unsolicited gift.[6] Perhaps, that is what Nebuchadnezzar had in mind by the food he provided here. If they had eaten this food, they would be more likely to comply with other requests in the future.

The most important grievance against eating the Babylonian food is that Scripture forbade it. In Leviticus, we learn that a Jew was forbidden to eat certain foods lest he defile himself: "You shall not make yourselves detestable with any swarming thing that swarms, and you shall not defile yourselves with them, and become unclean through them. For I am the LORD your God. Consecrate yourselves therefore, and be holy, for I am holy. You shall not defile yourselves with any swarming thing that crawls on the ground. For I am the LORD who brought you up out of the land of Egypt to be your God. You shall therefore be holy, for I am holy" (Leviticus 11:43-45, emphasis added).

Other dietary restrictions can be found in Deuteronomy and Isaiah: "Depart, depart, go out from there; touch no unclean thing; go out from the midst of her; purify yourselves, you who bear the vessels of the LORD" (Isaiah 52:11, emphasis added).

"Only be sure that you do not eat the blood. . . . You shall not eat it, that all may go well with you and with your children after you" (Deuteronomy 12:23, 25, emphasis added). Note that eating these foods would lead to a Jew being defiled.

Perhaps the Babylonians required this food as an attack upon the conscience of the Jews.

Furthermore, the food may have already been offered to a Babylonian god. Therefore, eating the meat would have been the equivalent of recognizing and honoring the god to which the food had been offered. For all practical purposes, Daniel, Hananiah, Mishael, and Azariah would have been denying the claims Jehovah had made as the one true God. The meat probably was not prepared in keeping with the food preparation regulations God had provided, which would have also been a method of defiling these Jews.

How did Daniel respond? "But Daniel resolved that he would not defile himself with the king's food, or with the wine that he drank. Therefore he asked the chief of the eunuchs to allow him not to defile himself" (Daniel 1:8). Daniel concluded that accepting this food would compromise his character. He resolved not to defile himself. He demonstrated remarkable wisdom as he discussed this matter with the Babylonian chief, who indicated that the consequence for failure in the training program would be death. Daniel 1:10 reads, "And the chief of the eunuchs said to Daniel, 'I fear my lord the king, who assigned your food and your drink; for why should he see that you were in worse condition than the youths who are of your own age? So you would endanger my head with the king.'"

Purity

The Bible says in 2 Timothy 2:21, "Therefore, if anyone cleanses himself from what is dishonorable, he will be a vessel for honorable use, set apart as holy, useful to the master of the house, ready for every good work." When Daniel, Hananiah, Mishael, and Azariah arrived in Babylon, they were standing in the largest city the world had seen until that time. They encountered great temptation. The real issue with the Babylonian food was whether these Judean youth would remain pure. The temptation with this food was an attempt to defile their hearts.

You will face similar challenges to compromise your purity. Your challenges will be more along the lines of 2 Timothy 2:22, "Flee youthful passions and pursue righteousness, faith, love, and peace, along with those who call on the Lord from a pure heart." Today most youth use alcohol and other drugs and find themselves immersed in the sexual hook-up culture. Should you choose to follow the biblical standard on sexual relationships, you will be in the minority. Between 60 percent and 80 percent of American college students have had intimate sexual experiences with people they do not even know.[7]

In fact, 70 percent of sexually active 12 to 21 year-olds reported having had uncommitted sex within the last year.[8] This behavior leads to serious consequences like assaults, sexually transmitted diseases, poor academic performance as well as other problems. In a sample of undergraduate students from Canada, 78 percent of women and 72 percent of men who had uncommitted sex reported a history of experiencing regret after such an encounter.[9] Had Daniel, Hananiah, Mishael, and Azariah ate the food described in Daniel 1 they would have experienced this same regret, which would have impeded their ability to influence others.

You should also expect challenges in the area of alcohol and other drugs. In a major study, 68.9 percent of college students reported drinking alcohol in the previous 30 days.[10] Each year, more than 1,825 college students die from alcohol-related accidents and nearly 600,000 are injured while drunk. Another 696,000 are assaulted by another student, who was drinking; and 97,000 are victims of alcohol-related sexual assault or date rape. Twenty-five percent of college students report academic consequences related to alcohol.[11]

And he said, "What comes out of a person is what defiles him. For from within, out of the heart of man, come evil thoughts, sexual immorality, theft, murder, adultery, coveting, wickedness, deceit, sensuality, envy, slander, pride, foolishness. All these evil things come from within, and they defile a person."
Mark 7:20-23

The temptation of sex, alcohol, and other drugs is an attempt to defile your heart and impede your ability to influence others. Should you choose to remain pure in these areas you will be following in the steps of Daniel, Hananiah, Mishael, and Azariah. When you make the decision to follow God and stay pure it can help you to keep from defiling yourself, and instead of becoming a victim of the culture, you can be used by God to influence the culture.

Do Hard Things

Difficult actions and choices often reveal a person's character. Prepare yourself for the ways your character will be assaulted in the future. Do the hard things to keep yourself pure from defilement. Good decisions tend to lead to more good decisions. Bad decisions tend to lead to more bad decisions.

If the four Hebrew men had said yes to Babylon by defiling themselves with Babylonian food, they would have placed themselves on a different trajectory in life, which would perhaps have led to further compromises and more distance from their identity and their God. They concluded that honoring God was more important than life itself.

Help yourself by developing godly habits (e.g., daily Bible reading, regular church attendance, fellowship with other believers, helping others). When stressed, people revert to old habits—even good ones. For a semester, researchers collected data on a group of undergraduates' eating, exercise, and other behaviors. When students were sleep-deprived, they were more likely to stick to old habits. Students who ate unhealthy pastries or doughnuts for breakfast ate even more during exams. Similarly, people who went to the gym were more likely to go to the gym when stressed.[12] If you are in the habit of reading your Bible you are more likely to keep doing that even in a crisis.

Certain in Resolve

Daniel was told failing to eat the food would endanger his life. Would this information dissuade Daniel from his resolution? No, Daniel and his friends were committed to the God they knew and loved. They remained firm in their resolve not to partake of this food.

Fortunately, these youth stayed firm. Daniel suggested they be allowed to eat vegetables rather than defile themselves. The steward that worked with them honored that request. They held onto their identity.

One Decision Leads to Another
What might have been

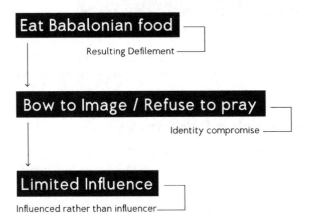

The lives of these four could have turned out very differently. It is unlikely they would have stood their ground at the fiery furnace some twenty years later. Perhaps decades later Daniel would have refused to pray to spare himself from the lion's den.

Key decisions affect the directions our lives take. How might this work in someone like yourself?

> ## Move to a new town and fail to begin attending church
>
> Resulting in break in fellowship
> with the people of God

> ## Fail to take time to read and study the Word
>
> Becoming spiritually anemic

> ## Choose ungodly friends
>
> Begin falling away from the LORD

The decisions you make today will set you on your life trajectory. If you make good decisions, it will become easier to continue on that path.

A Crisis Reveals a Relationship

Nebuchadnezzar had a dream that is recorded in Daniel 2. He became enraged when the wise men of the day could not tell him the meaning of the dream. He was convinced they were trying to deceive him and decided to kill the wise men and their families.

Arioch, the captain of the king's guard, approached Daniel to kill Daniel, Hananiah, Mishael, and Azariah. Daniel calmly asked Arioch for time. Then Daniel asked Hananiah, Mishael and Azariah to pray.

Daniel Prayed

Daniel began to pray "Blessed be the name of God forever and ever, to whom belong wisdom and might." (Daniel 2:20). Though

Daniel's life was at stake and he was under great stress, he prayed a prayer similar to Psalm 41:13, as well as a similar prayer offered by Job. This shows us that he turned to His Savior in his most difficult moments and recognized God's ability to take care of him. This was a habit. He enumerated the reasons why the name of God should be eternally blessed: "He changes times and seasons; he removes kings and sets up kings; he gives wisdom to the wise and knowledge to those who have understanding" (verse 21). The prayer distinguishes God from the idols of Babylon. God alone is the author of wisdom. Daniel gives God credit for his success.

Note how the prayer reminds us of statements Job made about the Lord. "With God are wisdom and might; he has counsel and understanding" (Job 12:13).

Daniel prays about the deep and secret things of God. He reveals what is in darkness. Again, note the similarities to Job.

"He reveals deep and hidden things; he knows what is in the darkness, and the light dwells with him" (verse 22).

"He uncovers the deeps out of darkness and brings deep darkness to light" (Job 12:22). Daniel recognized that it was God who could save him and God did. His relationship with God brought him through this difficulty and allowed him to survive and thrive in the midst of the crisis. The scriptural quality of his prayers indicates he had a deep relationship with the Lord, which strengthened him in the crisis.

Source of Strength

The source of this calmness became evident some 20 years later when Hananiah, Mishael, and Azariah refused to bow to an image Nebuchadnezzar had made. Daniel 3:7 tell us, "Therefore, as soon as all the peoples heard the sound of the horn, pipe, lyre, trigon, harp, bagpipe, and every kind of music, all the peoples, nations, and languages fell down and worshiped the golden image that King Nebuchadnezzar had set up."

Psychologist Robert Cialdini writes that peer pressure is more alluring when it seems that everyone is doing something. Here it seemed like everyone was bowing down to the image. That put the pressure upon Hananiah, Mishael, and Azariah to go along. Yet, they did not bow.

Nebuchadnezzar threatened Hananiah, Mishael, and Azariah, and gave them another chance to bow to the image. They remained firm. They said, "O Nebuchadnezzar, <u>we have no need to answer you in this matter</u>. If this be so, our God whom we serve is able to deliver us from the burning fiery furnace, and he will deliver us out of your hand, O king. <u>But if not</u>, be it known to you, O king, that we will not serve your gods or worship the golden image that you have set up'" (Daniel 3:16-18).

Basically, they say to the man who has the power to take their lives, "There is nothing to discuss here." Yet, this was not an idle threat. Nebuchadnezzar had killed people in this manner before (Jeremiah 29:22).

However, they responded by saying, "We have a God that can save us; we will not bow down to your god." In other words, "Our God may choose to save us, but if not, we will die remaining faithful to Him." Imagine how you would feel if someone tried to come between you and your best friend. Maybe they asked you to lie about them or do something that would hurt them in some way. That is an inkling of what was going on here. Nebuchadnezzar was trying to come between their relationships with God. That relationship was so strong that they would rather die than do something that might harm it. We all need that kind of relationship with God. This relationship allowed them to survive and thrive in Babylon. You too will survive and thrive in our culture if you have this kind of relationship with the Lord no matter what the world does to you.

Chapter 2

Be Substance

Don't succumb to the trend toward mediocrity. You may have seen the bumper sticker that says, "Mediocrity takes a lot less time, and most people won't notice the difference."

So, what is wrong with mediocrity? A lot!

Consider how we dislike mediocrity in our favorite sports teams. Years ago, my family and I watched the New York Yankees play the Texas Rangers. Whatever you think about the Yankees, you know they have a strong dislike for mediocrity. There was an attitude of expectation of a good performance, especially for some of their highly paid superstars.

At one point, New York was down 5-2. Yet, there was this sense that the Yankees could come back. Around the fifth inning, I went to get some snacks. Before I could come back, the Yankees had taken the lead and went on to win the game. Later that year, they won the World Series.

The next year we went to San Francisco to see the Giants play the Los Angeles Dodgers. They lost; in fact, it was the last of a three game sweep by the Dodgers. There was a sense of great displeasure. The next day, in the *San Francisco Chronicle*, we learned that the management made some big moves, and their first baseman, Buster Posey was moved to catcher. Before the changes, they were an okay (mediocre) baseball team. After the changes, they excelled. Later that year, they won the World Series.

Next, we saw the Chicago Cubs at Wrigley Field. They took an early lead only to eventually fall behind. You had a sense they were going to lose, that the lead was insurmountable. I went to get some snacks; and when I returned, they were even further behind. They lost. They didn't even make the wildcard playoffs that year though the team was decent—some would say mediocre.

Mediocrity is not any fun in sports. And when you really think about it, we do not like mediocre anything—cooking, service, or products. We especially dislike mediocrity when it comes to things that matter. Do you want a mediocre pilot in the cockpit of your airplane or a mediocre surgeon?

I think mediocrity is a sin. Proverbs 18:9 says, "Whoever is slack in his work is a brother to him who destroys." First Corinthians 10:31 states, "So, whether you eat or drink, or whatever you do, do all to the glory of God." If you are a Christian and you do mediocre work, it diminishes your influence and hurts the cause of Christ.

I once asked Duke University professor and researcher, Dr. Harold Koenig, how a believer could succeed in an environment when others were hostile toward their faith? He said, "Focus on doing a really good job." Do what you do well, or don't bother doing it at all.

Back to the Story

Second Kings 24:14 reveals King Nebuchadnezzar's plan of attack for Judah. "He carried away all Jerusalem and all the officials and all the mighty men of valor, 10,000 captives, and all the craftsmen and the smiths. None remained, except the poorest people of the land." Nebuchadnezzar took these young men as a way of controlling Judah. Rather than using a large occupying force, Nebuchadnezzar would weaken the nation he conquered by removing their talented and intelligent population, thereby using them to strengthen his own kingdom. In addition, the youth became quasi-hostages, a message to those left behind to cooperate since the regime had their children.[13]

Daniel 1:3-4 says, "Then the king commanded Ashpenaz, his chief eunuch, to bring some of the people of Israel, both of the royal family and of the nobility, youths without blemish, of good appearance and skillful in all wisdom, endowed with knowledge, understanding learning, and competent to stand in the king's palace, and to teach them the literature and language of the Chaldeans." The Babylonians chose Daniel, Hananiah, Mishael, and Azariah because they were young men of excellence. They were deemed to have aptitude so that they could be taught the literature and language of the Chaldeans. It has been noted by many that the Chaldean language may have been the most difficult language there was to learn in their day. Though they had prepared themselves to serve in the King of Judah's court, God was preparing them for Babylon. The abilities and knowledge they possessed were not developed in a day. It takes time to learn languages and comprehend literature. Apparently, they took advantage of the academic opportunities that came their way, which would later enable them to fulfill God's will for their lives.

The 10,000-Hour Rule

In his book, *Outliers*, Malcolm Gladwell chronicles the 10,000-hour rule by examining various individuals who have succeeded in remarkable ways. He emphasized how these individuals were prepared at a time when the environment was ripe for them to succeed. He chronicles the preparation of Bill Gates. Bill Gates attended a school where there was a computer club at a time when most colleges did not even have computer clubs. He reportedly "lived" in the computer room. Later he was given access to a computer center developed by programmers at the nearby University of Washington. He could walk to the University of Washington and use the computers at night and did so frequently between the hours of 3:00 and 6:00 a.m. When Gates dropped out of Harvard his sophomore year to start a software company, he'd been programming for 7 years. He had 10,000 hours of experience. He was prepared when the window of opportunity opened.[14]

You too need to take advantage of the opportunities that come your way. You may say: But I attend a bad school. Or I don't have enough money for books. Or we don't have those kinds of resources where we live. While that may be true—along with a host of other facts—everyone is given opportunities, talents, and gifts of various shapes and sorts. The key is to use rather than squander whatever opportunities you are given.

Ask yourself: What opportunities do I have? What talents do I possess? How can I use those for my good and God's glory?

Remember, you are not in this alone. You are called upon to faithfully prepare yourself but at the same time, it is God who is working in you to develop you into the person He wants you to be (Philippians 1:6). We see this in the lives of Daniel, Hananiah, Mishael, and Azariah. Though they had prepared well, and were faithful to refuse to defile themselves (Daniel 1:8), it was God who gave them the ability to succeed. In Daniel 1:19-20 we see the result, "...among all of them none was found like Daniel, Hananiah, Mishael, and Azariah. Therefore they stood before the king. And in every matter of wisdom and understanding about which the king inquired of them, he found them ten times better than all..."

Be Teachable

Nebuchadnezzar only wanted youth that were motivated to learn and willing to invest the time and energy needed to acquire the difficult language of the Chaldeans.

Seize the opportunity to learn. Never celebrate ignorance. When you realize you do not know something, learn about it. Educate yourself. Never brag about what you do not know, as if knowing things is shameful. Actually, be ashamed of ignorance, and let that motivate you to address deficiencies.

Also, just because you cannot see yourself using a subject in the future, don't assume you will not need it one day. I've heard students exclaim, "I'll never need Algebra!" They planned to be slack about the subject not knowing it will be on most college entrance exams regardless of their major.

How am I spending my time?

Activity	Percentage of Time
Study	
Skill acquisition	
Work	
Family	
Friends	
Bible Reading, Worship	
Social Media (Facebook, Twitter)	
Leisure (e. g., Movies, video games)	

I did the same thing. When I was young I thought, "I'll never need Spanish," and did not apply myself even though I took two years of Spanish. Today, I see Spanish speakers daily. At times, I've been alone in Spanish speaking countries unable to communicate. I squandered that opportunity and have lived to regret it.

Still, it is best to apply yourself to the subjects and tasks you enjoy because the more time you spend on something the better you tend to be at it. As you consider things you would like to study and do more, consider the way in which you are smart.

God may not expect you to obtain higher education or to be in the top of your class. But, He does expect you to use what He has given you. In Matthew 25:14-30 you can read about the parable of the talents. One man was given five talents, another two, and one man just one talent. In the story, Jesus explains that the master's key concern was what they did with their talents. Two of the three workers multiplied their talents. However, the man with only one talent failed to put it to use and was called a "wicked and slothful servant!" Ouch!

From the parable, we derive the principle "use it or lose it." God expects you to use whatever you have, so develop a mindset that values learning and wisdom. Apparently, Daniel, Hananiah, Mishael, and Azariah took advantage of the learning opportunities that came their way. They did not sit idly by consumed with boredom, and they were ready when they arrived in Babylon.

Boredom Is Not an Option

This means you never want to be bored. Wijinand van Tilburg, a psychologist at the University of Southampton, spent some time studying boredom. He concluded that boredom signals that what you are doing right now seems to be lacking purpose. People who are highly prone to boredom tend to perform poorly on tasks that require sustained attention, and it has been noted that chronic boredom can look a lot like depression.

Strangely, the number of people who say they are bored is on the rise. This is the case even though it is rare today to be at a point where we do not have anything to do. Most of us are bombarded by stimuli at our fingertips and can resort to television or other screens to alleviate boredom. In many ways, our electronic devices contribute to this problem by making us more likely to turn to them rather than our own activities when we have a moment with nothing to do. I encourage you to always have a project, something that stimulates your mind, a book you are reading, a language you are learning, a piece you are writing that you can begin work on when you have a few spare moments. Keep a little notebook in your back pocket and be prepared to spring into action when you have spare moments (e.g., stuck in line or traffic, waiting for a late plane, or a tardy teacher). I was once stuck in an elevator briefly. Some people panic in such situations. I pulled out my notebook and went to work. It helped me stay calm and gave me a few uninterrupted moments to work. Take advantage of these moments. Let it never be said of you that you are bored. The research indicates that the bored are more likely to abuse drugs, gamble, and overeat. Even worse, a study of British civil servants indicated that those who experienced a great deal of boredom were more likely to die young than those who were more engaged with the world! It was hypothesized that boredom leads people to take risks.[15] I doubt that Daniel, Hananiah, Mishael, and Azariah spent much time being bored. Instead, I suspect they spent their time developing skills. You too can do that. Rather than being bored, focus on developing a specific skill or expanding your knowledge of an area.

Be Prepared Academically

Daniel 1:17 says, "As for these four youths, God gave them learning and skill in all literature and wisdom, and Daniel had understanding in all visions and dreams." This Scripture literally says these four were knowers of knowledge. These guys worked hard and took advantage of the skills God gave them. If you have the chance, always take the more rigorous classes, read the harder books, and spend more time studying. Do what you can to take advantage of the academic opportunities that arise. When you have the opportunity, acquire skills. Learn how to do as much as you can. One day you will need that and much more.

Arguably, this knowledge saved the lives of these four as recorded in Daniel 2. Nebuchadnezzar was beginning the second year of his kingdom in March or April of 603 B.C., when he asked the wise men to interpret a dream he had. In Daniel 2, King Nebuchadnezzar ordered that all of the wise men of Babylon be destroyed (Daniel 2:12). Arioch, the captain of the king's guard began to seek out the wise men. He came to Daniel to kill him. Perhaps Arioch liked Daniel, or realized his value; at any rate, he did not immediately kill him. In fact, he paused and shared with Daniel the problem and allowed Daniel to ask the king to give him some time to work on the interpretation of the dream (Daniel 2:14-16).

Perhaps the ability Hananiah, Mishael, and Azariah had led Nebuchadnezzar to offer them a second chance after they refused to bow down to his golden image before he had them thrown into the fiery furnace. He questioned them (Daniel 3:14), and then gave Hananiah, Mishael, and Azariah another chance to bow down to the image, which they refused (Daniel 3:16-23) resulting in them being thrown into the fiery furnace.

Later, in Daniel 4 we see that Nebuchadnezzar had a problem, a dream he did not understand. After some time they brought Daniel to him. As Daniel walked in he exclaimed, "At last Daniel" when Daniel appeared (Daniel 4:8). Daniel possessed a God-given skill of dream interpretation. It is likely that Hananiah, Mishael, and Azariah also possessed God-given skills like administration. This competence, which God gave them and they faithfully developed, put them into a position to serve and help the people of Babylon. Remember, God has endowed you too with certain knowledge, areas that you would prefer to work in. Take some time to consider the way you are smart.

You may not have the ability to interpret dreams or the gift of administration but God has given you certain skills, or talents you need to develop. I fear we think too often of skills and intelligence as characteristics that are only useful in school settings. It may help to examine yourself with a theory of multiple intelligences developed years ago by Harvard psychologist Howard Gardner. He said every person is a unique blend of eight intelligences, and that people are intelligent in different ways.

Linguistic Intelligence: The ability to learn new languages and to use language. People with strengths in this area are good persuaders or storytellers and excel in occupations like writing, poetry, journalism, politics, and law.

Logical-Mathematical Intelligence: The capacity to analyze problems and carry out mathematical operations. The ability to detect patterns, reason deductively, and think logically. People with strengths in this area excel in science, research, mathematics, computer programming, accounting, and engineering.

Bodily-Kinesthetic Intelligence: The ability to control and coordinate complex physical movements. People with strengths in this area may be good at sports, acting, and gymnastics. People with strengths in this area excel in professions where balance and coordination are important like firefighting.

Visual-Spatial Intelligence: The ability to perceive objects in space and know where they should go. People with strengths in this area may be sculpturers, architects, navigators, interior designers, and engineers.

Interpersonal Intelligence: This is the capacity to understand others. People who excel in this area may become teachers, counselors, salespeople, marketing executives, and politicians.

Intrapersonal Intelligence: This is the ability to understand oneself. Writers and philosophers tend to excel in this area.

Musical Intelligence: The ability to work with patterns, rhythms and sounds. People with strengths in this area are good at singing and playing instruments, and remembering melodies. They excel in professions as musicians, composers, and music teachers.

Naturalistic Intelligence: This is the ability to relate to the natural environment. People who excel in this area often work as farmers or in mining or other outdoor activities.[16]

You could take an assessment at www.miresearch.org, which has been helpful in identifying the type of intelligence people possess. You can also explore your type at www.makeymakey.com.

Whatever your type of intelligence may be, remember it is the intelligence that God has given you. Therefore, commit to being a good steward of it. Look for ways to expand your knowledge with pertinent books, podcasts, and apps. Find the area where you tend to be the most intelligent and look for more activities you can do in these areas. Begin honing your skills and building your aptitude. Develop yourself into a knower of knowledge and develop a skill set that can solve problems. Make sure you are a good steward of the opportunities God has given you.

However, to excel in a particular area you will need to do some hard things like studying and working when others are asleep, playing, or wasting time. You must be a lifelong learner, or you will not impact your culture.

No Excuses

Think back to the incident of Nebuchadnezzar's dream problem (Daniel 2) that we examined earlier. What led Nebuchadnezzar to get angry enough to order the killing of the wise men? Perhaps he had an anger control problem. Probably, but I think his anger was triggered by the behavior of the Chaldeans. The Chaldeans were the political and religious gurus of their day. They were like the people you see on the cable news shows that seem to have all the answers. They could really put on a good show too. However, they were all fluff with no real stuff, and King Nebuchadnezzar was not fooled. Daniel 2:4, 8 reads, "Then the Chaldeans said to the king in Aramaic, 'O king, live forever! Tell your servants the dream, and we will show the interpretation.'...The king answered and said, 'I know with certainty that you are trying to gain time.'" The king did not care about symbolism; he had a need that could not be met with symbolism. Though many in our culture believe "image is everything," when problems arise, people get tired rather quickly of excuses and big shows.

> The Chaldeans answered the king and said,
> "There is not a man on earth who can
> meet the king's demand, for no great and
> powerful king has asked such a thing . . . The
> thing that the king asks is difficult . . .
> Daniel 2:10-11

I think the second reason Nebuchadnezzar became so angry was that the Chaldeans quit quickly. When the Chaldeans could not figure out the dream they made excuses ("the thing the king asks is difficult"), instead of pushing further for answers or searching for someone to assist.

We can learn from this error. When you encounter a difficult problem, instead of focusing on why something cannot be done, it is better to stop and think: How *can* this be done? Think: problem, alternatives, and solution. What needs to be done? How can it be done? What can I do to work through obstacles? Attack the problem like Daniel. Daniel asked for some time to look into the problem and asked God to help him. Remember, the same God who helped Daniel, helps you.

So instead of building your life around symbolism or fluff, prepare to be a problem solver. Acquire knowledge and develop skills that can be used to solve real problems in the future. That is the only way you will be prepared to influence the culture.

Grit

You might say the Chaldeans quit too easily because they lacked grit. Our culture also lacks grit. This is clear from studies of children of immigrants. According to a John Hopkins University study that tracked nearly 11,000 children, the best students (who later became the most successful young adults) were born in foreign countries and came to the United States before reaching their teens.[17] As these students become more like our culture, they become less successful. One culprit seems to be a lack of grit.

See Angela Lee Duckworth discuss Grit: The Key to Success www.ted.com/talks/angela_lee_duckworth_the_key_to_success_grit.html

Grit is defined as hard work, dedication, and perseverance that lead people to stick with a goal for years or decades until they succeed. It is an ingredient that predicts success ranging from who succeeds in the National Spelling Bee to the success of cadets at West Point and those who complete Special Forces Training. People who have grit do not mind working very hard. They are not worried about what they could be doing instead of working.[18] They keep at a thing until the job is done.

If you are going to be part of a faith that is increasingly unpopular, you had better have some grit, knowledge, and skills that make you valuable. People are more likely to tolerate you if you possess knowledge that can help them as we will see later in the lives of Daniel, Hananiah, Mishael, and Azariah. Remember, God knows the challenges that are coming your way, so take advantage of the opportunities He has given you.

Be Prepared Socially

In addition to preparing by developing your skills and acquiring knowledge to influence the culture, you will need some success with working with people. When teaching my students about intellectual assessment, I often give them a hypothetical vignette where they choose a neurosurgeon to remove a brain tumor. In this hypothetical example, the student somehow knows the IQs of the surgeons. I ask, "If you could choose between a neurosurgeon with a 120 IQ and one with 165, which would you choose?"

Immediately, my students say, "It depends. How well does the surgeon listen to me? How capable is he or she under pressure? How well does he or she adapt when a situation doesn't go as planned?"

Quickly it becomes obvious that whichever surgeon has the highest IQ is irrelevant. A 120 IQ will do the job intellectually. But, it will be social and emotional competence that provides the added benefit.

Unfortunately, many possess academic knowledge and skill, yet are ineffective because they have not prepared themselves socially. An example is the work of Lewis Terman, who followed 1,470 children into adulthood as they grew up in the San Francisco Bay area in the early 1900s. These children had IQs that ranged from 140-200, a score better than 99 percent of the people those instruments were normed on. Terman expected his students to succeed in remarkable ways. However, he was largely disappointed. These bright people were no more successful than the general population. There were some who were extremely successful, some that were moderately successful, and some that would be considered a failure. It did not turn out at all as Terman had expected.

In his book, *Outliers*, Malcolm Gladwell looked at Terman's work and noted that those who succeeded excelled academically as well as socially.[19] It was social competence (the ability to get along with and work well with others) that made the difference in their lives.

Dress for the Part

Appearance is a major aspect of social competence. My own experience tells me that how a person appears is very important. I've noted the importance of appearance for students who interview for selective programs at my university. I frequently see a student before an interview team interviews them. Most of the time an applicant that comes to an interview with a sloppy appearance does not get admitted. It is often assumed that they do not take the process seriously. There is a tendency to associate appearance with maturity and capability. Like it or not, how you look is important.

Notice how successful people dress. What does successful dress look like? Note how the president, CEO's, government leaders, and most major college coaches dress or the top achievers in particular fields. We all should dress for the part we want to play.

Notice the description of Daniel and his friends: "Youths without blemish, of good appearance and skillful in all wisdom" (Daniel 1:4a). Again later in that chapter: "Then let our appearance and the appearance of the youths who eat the king's food be observed by you, and deal with your servants according to what you see" (verse 13). Their appearance was important; it left an impression.

Joseph is another example from the Old Testament. When Joseph learned from prison that he would be going to meet Pharaoh, he immediately addressed his appearance to put his best foot forward. "Then Pharaoh sent and called Joseph, and they quickly brought him out of the pit. And when he had shaved himself and changed his clothes, he came in before Pharaoh" (Genesis 41:14).

So, look nice, neat, and modest. Go to iTunes U and type "Dress for Success" in the search feature. Listen to some of the podcasts from college career centers on dressing well.

Act the Part

Daniel 1:4b says that Daniel and his friends were "competent to stand in the king's palace," meaning they understood how to behave in the king's presence and palace. A certain decorum was required to stand or work in the king's palace; they understood and respected that. There is something to being able to act the part. Decorum is not valued as much today as in previous times.

Consider the decorum required for those who visit the *Tomb of the Unknown Soldier* in Arlington, Virginia. An example can be seen in the incident where a 30 year-old woman stood before a sign at the *Tomb of the Unknown Soldier* and photographed herself in an act of disrespect and posted it on Facebook.[20] The photo resulted in outrage and placed the woman's job in jeopardy.

In many ways, some people no longer know how to act. There is an atmosphere of increased rudeness and insensitivity toward others. In one poll, 79 percent of respondents said that a lack of respect and incivility is a serious problem in America. Sixty-one percent said it is getting worse.[21]

Be very careful about posts and pictures placed on Facebook, Pinterest, and Instagram. Also, think twice before tweeting. Be wise about

Netiquette

www.Netmanners.com
Netiquette resources: tinyurl.com/25qll
www.businessemailetiquette.com
Miss Netiquette's Guide to Twitter:
tinyurl.com/cyzb25u

social media. Ask: How would I like a future employer or admission counselor to see that? Sometimes the damage is not done by what you put on your own social media site, but it is the posts, comments, and pictures by your friends that can cause trouble.

College counselors with whom I work often recommend www.socioclean.com to students as they prepare to apply for jobs. This program analyzes social media sites and flags items potential employers might deem as offensive and therefore damage career prospects.

However, in the digital age, once something is out, it can never be completely deleted. So think twice before you send that angry email, post that picture, or write your political manifesto.

Who Gets Sued?

In his book, *Blink*, Malcolm Gladwell described the types of doctors who are sued by their patients. Surprisingly, a mistake made by the doctor is not the best predictor. Patients don't sue their doctors if they like them, even if they make mistakes. Most patients sue their doctors because they believe the doctor has bad bedside manners. How do doctors become liked by their patients? Doctors, who appear to care and have time for their patients, enjoy a better relationship with patients.

Medical researcher Wendy Levison looked at the conversations between doctors and their patients. She found that surgeons, who had never been sued, spent an average of three minutes longer with their patients than those who were sued (18.3 minutes versus 15 minutes). Taking their time with patients and giving them just three more minutes saved millions of dollars in malpractice suits.[22]

Be Likeable

And God gave Daniel <u>favor and compassion</u>
in the sight of the chief of the eunuchs.
Daniel 1:9

Go back to the beginning of this story when King Nebuchadnez-zar prescribed the diet which would have defiled Daniel, Hananiah, Mishael, and Azariah (Daniel 1). It appears from the beginning that these youth were liked. In fact, the Scripture says God gave Daniel this favor with his supervisors. Though you may be different from others it is important to remember that God is working not only in your life but in the life of others to accomplish His will. Proverbs 21:1 says, "The king's heart is a stream of water in the hand of the Lord; he turns it wherever he will." If you will be faithful to the Scripture, God will use you. Note that when Daniel had the problem with the diet he requested to be relieved of the requirement to eat the king's pre-scribed diet. The supervisor denied his request. Then Daniel went to another and approached him with a solution. In many ways Daniel was already applying Matthew 18 (the passage on dealing with con-flict) before it had been written. Though Daniel's initial request was rejected, he ultimately achieved his objective. Daniel was not trying to be confrontational, and he does not appear to have talked badly about his superiors or tried to embarrass them. He appears to have asked privately. When you encounter problems first discuss them pri-vately (Matthew 18) with the people involved. It is best to always ask: What do I want, and how might it be achieved? Daniel developed a solution that inconvenienced himself ("We will eat water and bread") rather than anyone else. He provided one of his superiors with a solu-tion and achieved his objective. The situation worked out.

Be Culturally Competent

Daniel, Hananiah, Mishael, and Azariah worked with individuals from many different backgrounds. Daniel 1:21 tells us they were in Babylon until the first year of King Cyrus, meaning they served under many different administrations: Nebuchadnezzar, Belshazzar, Darius, and Cyrus. The cultural competence of these four is seen in Daniel's service to multiple administrations from different nationalities. In order to survive and thrive in these different administrations these four had to work successfully with people that were very different from themselves. When Daniel, Hananiah, Mishael, and Azariah were taken to Babylon they were not just leaving their home behind. They were thrust into an environment that was filled with people that were very different from them.

Look back to the story in Daniel 3 when Nebuchadnezzar built a great statue and he brought those under his control to bow down to it. When Nebuchadnezzar held his ceremony to display his image, Daniel 3:2 notes that "King Nebuchadnezzar sent to gather the satraps, the prefects, and the governors, the counselors, the treasurers, the justices, the magistrates, and all the officials of the provinces to come to the dedication of the image." At this point in history, Nebuchadnezzar had conquered several countries. Many scholars believe the purpose of this endeavor was for Nebuchadnezzar to make sure all of these groups were under his authority. Daniel 3:4 says all "peoples, nations, and languages" bowed down. This indicates that these four regularly interacted with all kinds of people. The Chaldeans noted that Hananiah, Mishael, and Azariah did not bow down to the image and in Daniel 3:12 said, "There are certain Jews whom you have appointed over the affairs of the province of Babylon: Shadrach, Meshach, and Abednego." Since Hananiah, Mishael, and Azariah were leaders in Babylon, they must have been quite effective working with different types of people. Daniel too possessed this ability, which will become even more obvious later as Daniel will serve under Darius the king of Persia, the nation that will defeat Babylon. We too need this ability. How culturally competent are you? What do you know about the cultures of different groups of people?

Rate Your Cultural Competence

- I view people that look/speak/believe different than I as "those people."
- I am unconcerned with understanding people that look/speak/believe different than I.
- I am unconcerned with getting along with people that look/speak/believe different than I.

If you answered yes, to any of these statements you need some help. Remember, you have far more in common with someone who is a believer even though they may look very different from you. It is important to view all people as important if you hope to reach out to them and help them. If you are unconcerned about getting to know people that are different from you then you are failing to answer God's call to love your neighbor as yourself.

How can you grow in the area of cultural competence? Think about how people in a particular culture feel when certain events transpire. Consider what you would say to people from different cultures. Seek opportunities to interact with and learn from different cultures. Try to put yourself in their shoes and refrain from saying things that might be hurtful. If someone from a different culture seems offended by something you say, rather than becoming defensive, try to see the issue from his or her perspective.

It should be noted that when it comes to cultural competence, we tend to overrate our ability so we all probably need a lot of help here because this is an important area in which to excel if you are to positively impact the culture. When you talk about being culturally sensitive, some people protest and say they have no desire to be politically correct. I'm not concerned with political correctness, but we want to make sure we are spiritually correct. Fortunately, the Scripture gives us great guidance about how to increase our cultural competence.

Consider the admonition of the Apostle Paul: "If possible, so far as it depends on you, live peaceably with all" (Romans 12:18). What does this mean? How was Paul culturally competent? First Corinthians 9:19-23 explains, "For though I am free from all, I have made myself a servant to all, that I might win more of them. To the Jews I became as a Jew.... To those under the law I became as one under the law.... To those outside the law I became as one outside the law.... To the weak, I became weak.... I have become all things to all people, that by all means I might save some. I do it all for the sake of the gospel, that I may share with them in its blessings."

Note that Paul took on the perspective of others so that he could positively influence them.

Paul admonished us to respect our leaders and he himself was successful in reaching many in Caesar's household (Philippians 4:22).

As a general principle, it is best to think about what you are trying to accomplish before you make statements that might offend someone. Be especially careful when it comes to political views. Political views can be very polarizing so be very careful before you disparage a particular candidate or public official. Though you may have the right to do so it is important to remember how you are trying to influence people toward Christ. Proverbs 18:19 indicates, "A brother offended is more unyielding than a strong city, and quarreling is like the bars of a castle." Some of the hard teachings of the gospel can be offensive enough (e.g., Jesus is the only way to heaven) without us contributing our own idiosyncrasies. So try to avoid offending people about less important matters. Before you make a statement, ask: Will this statement or argument impede my ability to witness to certain groups of people?

43

The Culturally Competent Apostle

Consider how the cultural competence of the Apostle Paul enabled him to work with all kinds of very different people. In Acts 13:43 we see Paul ministering to Jews, "...many Jews and devout converts to Judaism followed Paul and Barnabas, who, as they spoke with them, urged them to continue in the grace of God." Later in Acts 16 we find Paul answering the call to minister to pagan Europeans in Macedonia. He ministered to leaders like the Philippian Jailor (Acts 16:25-34), as well as the cultural elite (Acts 17:22-34) in his day. When Paul addressed the Areopagus at Athens, it was akin to walking onto a college campus and speaking to the professors in an assembly. Paul also ministered to Jewish leaders (Acts 24:24-27; Acts 25-26), military leaders (Acts 27:43), and the wealthy (Philemon). Paul also admonished us to respect government leaders, though ironically it appears one of those leaders ordered his death. Later in Philippians 4:22 we see that even members of Caesar's household became believers.

So do not attack someone (even government leaders) just because everyone else does. It is also wise to refrain from attacking an easy target or someone who is particularly unpopular at the moment. It does not tend to garner the respect of others. Your conversation will be very different from your peers as Colossians 4:6 teaches us, "Let your speech always be gracious, seasoned with salt, so that you may know how you ought to answer each person." As you deal with others be honest, but be wise. Always keep the big idea in mind. Being kind and having time for others will give you the opportunity to influence them toward Christ. We are trying to reach people with the gospel, and it helps to be liked.

Be Prepared Emotionally

Intellectual competence and social competence are necessary to influence the culture. However, you will not achieve your objective without emotional maturity. Are you easily disappointed? Do you find yourself especially sensitive to criticism? Are you fearful?

Daniel Goleman's classic book, *Working with Emotional Intelligence*, was derived by analyzing what more than 120 companies wanted in their employees. Sixty-seven percent of the competencies desired were emotional in nature. He defines emotional competence as self-awareness (knowledge of your own abilities and shortcomings), self-regulation (able to manage emotional distress), motivation (goal oriented and able to overcome setbacks), empathy (aware of how others think and feel), and social skills (able to work well with other people). Business leaders indicated a desire for employees who listened well, were able to get past setbacks, were motivated, were able to get along well with others, and were willing to contribute to others.[23]

Be Calm

The emotional competence of Daniel, in particular, has been seen in the incident from Daniel 2 when Nebuchadnezzar ordered the killing of the wise men because the Chaldeans were unable to tell Nebuchadnezzar his dream. Daniel 2:13-14 says, "So the decree went out, and the wise men were about to be killed; and they sought Daniel and his companions, to kill them. Then <u>Daniel replied with prudence and discretion to Arioch</u>, the captain of the king's guard, who had gone out to kill the wise men of Babylon."

Daniel, Hananiah, Mishael, and Azariah had to be cool and calm under pressure. Not only did they survive the traumatic overthrow of their nation and subsequently stand up for their beliefs regarding diet, but they also, encountered a death threat when King Nebuchadnezzar was upset because the wise men could not interpret his dream (Daniel 2:13). Daniel, Hananiah, Mishael, and Azariah were considered wise men. Nebuchadnezzar ordered their execution. When someone visits you with the task of killing you, well, that can elevate your stress level. Note that Daniel replied with "prudence and discretion" (Daniel 2:14), and calmly asked, "why is this so urgent?" (Daniel 2:15). Daniel slowed this crisis down by asking Arioch a question, he also asked that he be given some time to work on the problem. Arioch allowed Daniel to make his request to the king and Daniel was given more time to work on an answer to the dream (Daniel 2:16). Next, Daniel enlisted the help of his godly friends (Hananiah, Mishael, and Azariah), and they prayed about the problem (Daniel 2:17-18). God gave Daniel the dream and its interpretation (Daniel 2:19). Daniel used the situation as an opportunity to tell Nebuchadnezzar about the one true God ("There is a God in heaven who reveals mysteries" Daniel 2:28). A crisis became an opportunity, and Daniel and his friends were catapulted forward (Daniel 2:48-49).

We can learn from this event. When you find yourself in danger, you want to slow things down. This allows you to calm down a bit and to think about an appropriate course of action. Similarly, if you can be cool during a crisis you will find that many of these crises become opportunities to help and influence others.

To succeed you too will need to learn to deal well with stress and pressure. You will do this by allowing yourself to be in stressful situations and dealing well with them. As you do, your emotional intelligence should grow.

Another example of emotional intelligence is in Daniel 5 in the famous story of the handwriting on the wall. Nebuchadnezzar is no longer on the scene. King Belshazzar who is throwing a big feast with thousands of people (Daniel 5:1) has replaced him. He is using vessels that Nebuchadnezzar had taken from the temple in Jerusalem. This was very disrespectful to the God of Daniel. During the party, the king became very frightened as a finger began to write on the wall (Daniel 5:5-6). Daniel is not at this party and it appears that he is not held with the same esteem that he experienced in the kingdom of Nebuchadnezzar. One of the big tests of emotional intelligence is in how you deal with disappointment, slights, and those who devalue you. Instead of pouting over these apparent slights, Daniel prepared to help when he was called to assist Belshazzar. How can we deal with disappointment or being devalued? The passage in Daniel 5 reinforces the principle that people will eventually seek out the help of those who are competent once the situation gets desperate enough. Bad things will happen to you so you must be prepared to deal with them. The Word of God will be a comfort to you, and you will need to develop techniques like walking, exercising, or praying to help you cope. But you must learn to deal with discouragement, which is a key to emotional competence.

Be Prepared Spiritually

Academic, social, and emotional competences are necessary. However, competence begins with the Lord. Proverbs 1:7 says, "The fear of the LORD is the beginning of knowledge; fools despise wisdom and instruction."

We have already discussed how Daniel, Hananiah, Mishael, and Azariah must have read the Hebrew Bible and its prominence in their prayer life. But it is important to note that those who knew them acknowledged that they were spiritually mature.

Nebuchadnezzar spent enough time with Daniel to know he was spiritually mature. In Daniel 4, another dream Nebuchadnezzar had is recorded. We will look at this closer later but it alarmed Nebuchadnezzar (Daniel 4:5). The Chaldeans were unable to give the answer to the dream so Nebuchadnezzar turned to Daniel. When Daniel arrived, Daniel 4:8 records the king's words, "At last Daniel came in before me—he who was named Belteshazzar after the name of my god, and in whom is the spirit of the holy gods—and I told him the dream." Nebuchadnezzar, a prideful and oppressive man, even saw the spiritual competence of Daniel. He still called him Daniel (meaning, "God is Judge") though he noted he had changed his name.

Decades later, Nebuchadnezzar's wife spoke about Daniel as the nation faced another crisis: "There is a man in your kingdom <u>in whom is the spirit of the holy gods</u>. In the days of your father, light and understanding and wisdom like the wisdom of the gods were found in him, and King Nebuchadnezzar, your father—your father the king—made him chief of the magicians, enchanters, Chaldeans, and astrologers" (Daniel 5:11).

Even Daniel's enemies recognized his faith. They realized his faith was the only thing they could use against him if they wished to attack him: "Then these men said, 'We shall not find any ground for complaint against this Daniel <u>unless we find it in connection with the law of his God</u>'" (Daniel 6:5).

After his faith was used against him, Darius too, described Daniel's faith though the ruler cast Daniel into a den of lions: "Then the king commanded, and Daniel was brought and cast into the den of lions. The king declared to Daniel, '<u>May your God, whom you serve continually, deliver you!</u>'" (Daniel 6:16). These spiritual competencies were developed in their youth and served them throughout their lives. We too can develop these competencies.

Dr. Robert Picirilli is a modern day example of a spiritually competent person. In the videos linked at survivingculture.com he first discusses how these competencies helped him early in his life as he committed himself to follow Christ. Later he discussed how these competencies have helped him even as he has transitioned into older age. May you too be a man or woman of faith. May you spend time in prayer to God and reading His Word so that it is obvious to others that you have been with God (Acts 4:13).

Chapter 3

Be Yourself

God made you for a particular purpose. Ephesians 2:10 says, "We are his workmanship, created in Christ Jesus for good works, which God prepared beforehand, that we should walk in them." This means God has gifted you to do what He wants you to do. Psalm 139:13-14 says, "For you formed my inward parts, you knitted me together in my mother's womb: I will praise you for I am fearfully and wonderfully made. Wonderful are your works; my soul knows it very well." So God was involved in every detail of who you are. From your interest, abilities, and desires, all the way down to your DNA. God has prepared you for the task He wants you to perform.

In his book *Creativity*, Mihaly Csikszentmihalyi examined the lives of 91 people who were at the top of their field. These people were known for their creativity. Csikszentmihalyi noted that before one could excel in an area he or she needed to be extremely proficient in that content. Today people often think of creativity as something that happens suddenly, Csikszentmihalyi has noted that real creativity is usually the result of years of work.[24]

See Mihaly Csikszentmihalyi discuss flow at: www.ted.com/talks/mihaly_csikszentmihalyi_on_flow.html

This observation is similar to the 10,000-hour rule discussed in Chapter 2 that indicates one must spend a lot of time in an area to know it well before arriving at a level of creativity.

God made some of you to excel in math. He has endowed you with ability. To truly excel and be a good steward of this ability you must take many rigorous courses in mathematics (e.g., geometry, trigonometry, and calculus). Since God made you this way, in addition to coursework, you will be thinking about and doing math when you are not taking classes. You might find yourself thinking about math in your spare time.

If your field is history, in addition to coursework, you will probably have history books in your book bag that you will read in your spare time and history podcasts on your MP3 player. This is the 10,000-hour rule at work. To be good, you must spend your time on the things you love to do.

In another book called *Flow*, Csikszentmihalyi discussed happiness. He stated that it is a mistake to pursue happiness itself, and that those who tend to be truly happy are those who engage in activities for enjoyment and satisfaction that totally engage their minds.[25] One might conclude from his work that one will only be truly happy when he or she is engrossed in the activities he or she were created to perform or become the person God has made him or her to be.

The Bible teaches us that if you delight in God He will give you the desires of your heart (Psalm 37:4). What does that mean? Will God agree to your video gamer aspirations? It means as you identify with Christ as your Lord, your only hope of salvation, that He redeems you, turning your self-centered, sinful desires into a heart, a life that finds its most joy in pursuing God's desires for you. That is when a person settles into what he or she was created to be. God makes you want what He wants you to want.

Step 1. Present Your Life to God

Ask: Is there anything I would not do even if I felt God wanted me to do it? Is there anywhere I would not go even if I felt God wanted me to go there? Romans 12:1 says, "...present your bodies as a living sacrifice, holy and acceptable to God, which is your spiritual worship."

Therefore, the first thing you must do is to give your life to God with the attitude, "I will go where You want me to go, and do whatever You want me to do." You cannot skip this step.

Too many people put parameters around God as the Old Testament prophet Jonah did. Apparently, Jonah was willing to serve God, but on his own terms. God instructed Jonah to go to minister to Nineveh (Jonah 1:2). He was unwilling to serve in Nineveh, which was an enemy of Israel, and actually went in the opposite direction (Jonah 1:3). Contrast his attitude with the attitude of Daniel. Daniel prepared to serve in Judah but was called to serve in Babylon (the enemy of Judah). Daniel's love for God and his relationship with God allowed him to serve faithfully in Babylon.

Step 2. Assess Yourself

The next step is to conduct a sober or serious assessment upon yourself. Romans 12:3 says one should not "think of himself more highly than he ought to think, but to think with sober judgment, each according to the measure of faith that God has assigned." Often, when I have asked college students or young workers why they selected their major or a particular job they say, "That's where the money is" or "My friends suggested it." It would be wiser to choose your field or job because you were made for it. If you are good at something and like it, you are going to excel. This means you must find the strengths God has given you.

Find Your Strengths

The key to success is determining what God made you to do and going to do it. Therefore, it is critical to find the strengths God has given you. As you think of the kind of work you will do or how you will spend your time, ask: What am I good at? Start by looking at your grades. What are your favorite academic subjects? What academic subjects do you dislike? What is your work history? What are your hobbies? What club and church activities do you most enjoy? Based on your own assessment, what are your top three favorite subjects? What are your least favorite subjects? We cannot ignore the subjects we dislike. In order to be well rounded, we will need a certain level of proficiency in broad areas.

Find free online courses and books of interest to you at www.openculture.com

However, once you find that you are better suited for certain areas, it is wise to spend more time there. For example, let us say your grades and interest are high in the social study subjects, but you dislike math. It would then be wise to explore these areas by taking as many rigorous courses (e.g., US Government, European History, and Economics) as you can.

To get a better understanding of what you are good at take a look at your latest achievement test results. Where did you score the highest? The lowest?

To understand what the scores mean look at two terms. The first is a stanine. These scores help you see how your abilities on certain subjects compare to other students your age. Scores of 1 to 3 indicate that you are not as strong in these areas as other students. Scores of 4 to 6 indicate that you are

Looking for an Aptitude Test?
PSAT: www.CollegeBoard.com
SAT: www.SAT.CollegeBoard.org
ACT: www.ACT.org
ASVAB: http://official-asvab.com

like most people in these areas. Scores of 7 to 9 indicate that you do better in this area than most people. Another way to understand these scores is to look at the percentile rank (PR). This number tells you specifically how your skill level in an area compares to others. For example, if you score in the 35th percentile on an area, this means you did as well as or better than 35 percent of the norming population on this instrument. This would mean this area is not a strength for you. On the other hand, if you scored in the 65th percentile (as well as or better than 65 percent of the norming population), this would be a strength for you. In addition, look at the scaled scores, which can help you monitor your progress from one year to another.

When you find yourself excelling in an area, spend more time in those areas. If your school does not offer courses in some of these subjects, talk to your school counselor or principal about taking some of these courses at a community college or online.

Looking for AP courses your school does not have?
Go to https://apstudent.collegeboard.org/

The research indicates that taking high-level mathematics courses like pre-calculus in high school increases the likelihood of success in college. Taking Advanced Placement (AP) or International Baccalaureate courses increases the likelihood of success in college even if students fail the end of course exam. The more of these types of courses taken in high school the more likely a student persists at their four-year or two-year institution. A rigorous high school curriculum is key to success.[26]

You can also assess your strengths by looking at aptitude tests like the Preliminary Scholastic Assessment Test (PSAT), Scholastic Assessment Test (SAT), and American College Testing (ACT). These instruments are usually used as a means to enter a program of study, but they too can provide a good indication of your ability. However, these tend to be limited to your verbal, quantitative, and analytical skills.

Ask your school counselor about taking the Armed Services Vocational Aptitude Battery (ASVAB). The ASVAB will provide a wider range of skill areas.

Step 3. What are you like?

Psalm 139:15-16 reads, "My frame was not hidden from you, when I was being made in secret, intricately woven in the depths of the earth. Your eyes saw my unformed substance; in your book were written, every one of them, the days that were formed for me, when as yet there was none of them." This indicates that your ability to do things was given to you by the Lord so there will be tasks you are better at performing than others because God made you that way. Every person is different with different functions within the body of Christ.

> *Now concerning spiritual gifts, brothers, I do not want you to be uninformed.* *...For to one is given through the Spirit the utterance of wisdom, and to another the utterance of knowledge according to the same Spirit, to another faith by the same Spirit, to another gifts of healing by the one Spirit, to another the working of miracles, to another prophecy, to another the ability to distinguish between spirits, to another various kinds of tongues, to another the interpretation of tongues. ...And God has appointed in the church first apostles, second prophets, third teachers, then miracles, then gifts of healing, helping, administrating, and various kinds of tongues.*
> *1 Corinthians 12:1, 8-10, 28*

> *Having gifts that differ according to the grace given to us, let us use them: if prophecy, in proportion to our faith; if service, in our serving; the one who*

*teaches, in his teaching; the one who exhorts, in his
exhortation; the one who contributes, in generosity;
the one who leads, with zeal; the one who does acts
of mercy, with cheerfulness.*
Romans 12:6-8

What do you do well with minimal effort? What kind of tasks do you find yourself doing and lose track of time? What are you like?

When I was a boy, I could not understand why I had so much trouble playing baseball. I seemed good at most sports, but when it came to baseball, I could not throw. It bothered me. I had been given a baseball glove and could field well with it; I just could not throw very far. One day I went to my backyard and threw two baseballs. I threw the first ball with my right hand as hard as I could. It did not go far. Then I threw with my left hand. The ball went out of the yard and over a big fence. Soon after, I met a man who lent me a left-handed glove. I had never seen a glove for left-handed people, but that day I realized how liberating it can be to know what you are really good at and be able to do what you were made to do.

In a similar fashion, you have a personality, interests, and abilities God gave you when He created you. When you operate in the areas where you are gifted, you tend to be more successful, happier, and more influential.

For example, do you like working with people or would you rather work alone? Do you tend to focus on what could be or are you more concerned with the here and now? Do you make decisions based on logic or find yourself making decisions based on your concerns for someone else? Do you make decisions quickly, or do you feel like you need as much information as possible before coming to a conclusion? It is important to discover the way God made you to be and to operate in that realm.

Interests

Some people enjoy working with machinery and working alone while others prefer to be with other people and might even struggle to change the pressure in the tires of a car. These preferences are a result of a person's interests.

Psychologist John Holland studied people and their occupations and concluded that people have interest types, which can be described as realistic, investigative, artistic, social, enterprising, and conventional.

In this next section I have provided descriptions of each interest type. Take time to read each one carefully and then examine the chart that corresponds with each type. Before you move on to another interest type be sure to rate your strengths in each area.

Realistic

People with the realistic type tend to enjoy activities requiring physical, mechanical, and spatial abilities. They prefer concrete rather than abstract tasks. They are often described as quiet and tend to value freedom, ambition, and self-control. They tend to gravitate to occupations such as engineering, navigation, plumbing, and other service occupations like electricians and technicians. Inventors tend to be realistic. Thomas Edison and Mike Rowe are good examples of the realistic type.

Realistic Types[27]

Academic Subjects	Value	Activities	Majors and Programs	Typical Occupations
Math	Quiet	Agricultural clubs	Agriculture	Agriculture
		Intramural Sports	Animal Science	Computer Repair
		ROTC	Automotive Services	Law Enforcement
			Aviation	Military Activity
			Electronics	Outdoors
			Engineering	Transportation
			Forestry	
			Heating, Air Conditioning and Refrigeration	
			Horticulture	
			Medical Technology	
			Welding	

Rate the strength of your realistic characteristics.

Low   Medium   High

<_____>

Investigative

Investigative people tend to like science, medicine, mathematics, and research. They are often described as reserved, curious, thorough, analytical, and scholarly. They tend to value wisdom and logic. These people tend to gravitate to occupations in the sciences and occupations that require the highest educational levels. Examples include laboratory technician, computer programmer, and electronics worker. Albert Einstein and Dr. Benjamin Carson are good examples of the investigative type.

Investigative Types[28]

Academic Subjects	Value	Activities	Majors and Programs	Typical Occupations
Science	Curiosity	Chess Club Science Club (Astronomy, Geology) Volunteer for research projects	Antrhropology Archeology Biology Botany Chemistry Computer Information Systems Health Sciences Mathematics Meteorology Paramedics Social Sciences Zoology	Engineering Health Care Research Science

Rate the strength of your realistic characteristics.

Low   Medium   High

< _____ >

Artistic

Artistic people tend to like activities involving self-expression, communication, and culture. They are often described as careless, disorderly, dreamy, introspective, sensitive, sophisticated, and creative. They tend to value beauty and imagination. These people tend to gravitate to occupations involving music, writing, and art. T. S. Eliot and Pablo Picasso are good examples of the artistic type.

Artistic Types[29]

Academic Subjects	Value	Activities	Majors and Programs	Typical Occupations
Language classes	Introspection	Foreign Language Clubs	Advertising	Advertising
Art		Musical Group	Architecture	Architecture
Drama		Student Publications	Broadcasting	Culinary Arts
		Theater Productions	Creative Writing	Entertainment
			Design	Writing
			English	Video/Film
			Fine Arts	
			Mass Communication	
			Music	
			Education	

Rate the strength of your realistic characteristics.

Low   Medium   High

< _____ >

Social

Social people tend to like activities involving people, teamwork, and community. They are often described as capable, enthusiastic, friendly, kind, warm, and persuasive. These people tend to gravitate to occupations like teaching and counseling. Leaders tend to be social. Most politicians and pastors are good examples of the social type.

Social Types[30]

Academic Subjects	Value	Activities	Majors and Programs	Typical Occupations
Psychology	Cooperation	Intramural Sports	Child Development	Child Care
Business		Resident Hall Advisor	Counseling	Counseling
		Tutoring	Criminology	Education
		Organizations	Education	Healt Care
			Hearing and Speech Sciences Nursing	Tourism
			Public Health	
			Recreation	
			Religious Studies	

Rate the strength of your realistic characteristics.

Low   Medium   High

< _____ >

Enterprising

Enterprising people tend to like activities involving selling, managing, and persuading. They are often described as aggressive, extroverted, and popular. These people tend to gravitate to occupations involving business and politics. Leaders tend to be enterprising; Henry Ford, Andrew Carnegie, and Steve Jobs are good examples of the enterprising type.

Enterprising Type[31]

Academic Subjects	Value	Activities	Majors and Programs	Typical Occupations
Government	Adventure	Business	Business	Business
History		Student Organizations	Cosmetology	Insurance
			Culinary	Investments
		Campus Political Groups	Training	Legal Services
			Finance	Marketing
		Student Government Association	Government	Management
			History	Real Estate
			Insurance	Sales
			Management	
			Marketing	
			Political Science	
			Prelaw	
			Public Administration	

Rate the strength of your realistic characteristics.

Low   Medium   High
<_____>

Conventional

Conventional people tend to like organizing, setting up procedures, and keeping records. They are often described as practical, accurate, stable, meticulous, precise, and efficient. These people tend to gravitate to occupations involving data management, accounting, and investing. Experts in finance and commerce tend to be conventional. John D. Rockefeller is a good example of the conventional type.

Conventional Type[32]

Academic Subjects	Value	Activities	Majors and Programs	Typical Occupations
Math	Stability	Financial Aid Advising	Accounting	Accounting
		Office Assistant	Banking	Banking
			Financial Planning	Bookkeeping
		Secretary or Treasurer of a Student	Office Systems	Data Management
		Organization	Mathematics	Office Work
		Math or Statistics Tutor	Statistics	Tax Consulting

Rate the strength of your realistic characteristics.

Low   Medium   High

< _____ >

So what type are you? Find out and spend more time on those tasks, being the person God created you to be.

How to find your type
Career Key: www. careerkey.org
Self-Directed Search:
www.self-directed-search.com
Also, consider the Kuder: www.kuder.com

Personality

God also made you with a particular type of personality, and you are more likely to excel if you can work in the areas that allow you to express yourself. What kind of personality do you have?

It can be helpful to consider four types assessed by an instrument called the Myers-Briggs Type Indicator (MBTI).

How do you find your type?
See a career counselor to take the Myers-Briggs Type Indicator.
Go online to view the Keirsey:
www. Keirsey.com

If you are in college, you might be able to take the MBTI in your career-counseling center. The MBTI is based on the work of Carl Jung. One's type can also be assessed for a fee using the Keirsey Temperament Sorter (KTS).

Extraversion or Introversion

People tend to be extraverted or introverted. Extraverted people are energized when they work in groups and are able to be with other people. They may like public speaking and occupations like selling and politics. They like activity and tend to talk more than they listen.

Learn more about the Myers Briggs Type Indicator at www.myersbriggs.org

Introverts on the other hand do their best work when they are alone or in small groups. If they are working on a project with other people, they will need some down time to be rejuvenated once the project is complete. They like occupations like science and writing or anything involving introspection. They listen more than they talk.

In our culture, introverts are not valued as much as others are though our culture needs them.

Preference Types	Occupational Areas[33]
Sensing and Thinking	Surgery, law, accounting, working with machinery
Sensing and Feeling	Nursing, teaching, social work, selling, service jobs
Intuition and Feeling	Teaching, preaching, adverstising, counseling, writing, and research
Intuition and Thinking	Science, computing, mathematics, and finance

Sensing or Intuition

People who are sensing tend to focus on facts and take in information using their five senses. Sensing types are oriented toward the present; they value common sense and practicality.

Intuitive types tend to take in information from patterns and focus on what could be. They value imagination and ingenuity. They tend to be able to read between the lines.

Thinking or Feeling

Thinking types tend to look at things logically and make decisions based on logic. You might say they value truth over tact. Feelers tend to think about the impact of a particular decision.

Feelers tend to be tender minded and subjective. Sometimes people who are thinkers may be perceived as harsh while feelers might be viewed as a push over.

Judging or Perceiving

Judgers like a planned and organized approach to life. Judgers are quick to make decisions. They tend to be on time and like organization. They want to see things resolved, like fixed deadlines and are product oriented.

Perceivers do not wish to miss anything. They may be late or considered messy and are slower to make a decision. Perceivers like flexibility and prefer to keep their options open. They are process oriented and often miss deadlines. To learn more check out Tieger and Barron-Tieger's *Do What You Are*, and Kroeger & Thueson's *Type Talk at Work*.

A Personal Profile
What are my top 3 academic subjects?

1.
2.
3.

What are my top 3 interest areas?

1.
2.
3.

What is your personality like:

E or I

S or N

T or F

J or P

My Top Occupations

1. _____

Key Tasks Performed: _____

Education & Training Required: _____

2. _____

Key Tasks Performed: _____

Education & Training Required: _____

3. _____

Key Tasks Performed: _____

Education & Training Required: _____

4. _____

Key Tasks Performed: _____

Education & Training Required: _____

5. _____

Key Tasks Performed: _____

Education & Training Required: _____

Step 4: Sum It Up

O*NET is a very helpful website produced by the United States Department of Labor (www.onetonline.org). There you can explore occupations tied to your personal profile. For example, if your favorite subject is history, type "history" in the occupational search slot. Also, select advanced search and knowledge. You can do a similar search by selecting abilities. For example, type in "writing" and look at the occupational choices that are provided. Identify occupations that would be of interest to you and explore the tasks performed in this job as well as the skills and education required to perform them. Do the same search again, but this time type your top interest into the occupational search slot and under the advanced search option, choose "interest." Try to make a list of ten possible occupations.

Now go to the Occupational Outlook Handbook (www.bls. gov/ooh), which is also operated by the

Check out the U.S. Department of Labor website that helps you match skills to an occupation: http://mynextmove.dol.gov

United States Department of Labor. You can explore the occupational groups there (e.g., arts and design, business and financial, healthcare, military, sales). What are the core tasks performed by people in these occupations? What type of training is required for this occupation? If the occupation requires college, what majors are usually required? Is graduate or professional school necessary? Pay special attention to the tasks, condition, location, and benefits of each occupation.

Step 5: How Do You Get There?

Once you narrow down some possible occupations, consider interviewing some people in those positions. Use the questions below as a starting point for the interview:

1. How did you obtain this position?
2. What is a typical day like for you?
3. What do you like most about this position?
4. What do you dislike about this position?
5. What are some of the biggest challenges facing your industry?
6. What professional associations should I be connecting with?
7. How do you see the industry changing over the next 10 years?[34]
8. How did you prepare for this career?
9. What are the opportunities for advancement in this field?

Paying for College

Going 2 College: www.going2college.org
Provides resources to explore, plan, and examine how to pay for college.

College Savings Plans Network:
www.collegesavings.org
Provides strategies for getting financial aid and being admitted into college.

FAFSA Forecaster: www.FAFSA4caster.ed.gov
Examines options for paying for college.

Federal Student Aid: www.studentaid.gov
U.S. Department of Education site where you can see if you qualify for financial aid and apply for aid.

Choosing a College

College Affordability and Transparency Center:
http://collegecost.gov
U.S. Department of Education site that examines the cost, graduation, and employment rate of colleges.

College Navigator: http://nces.ed.gov/collegenavigator
Institute for Education Sciences site that allows you to make comparisons between colleges you are considering.

National Survey of Student Engagement:
http://Nsse.iub.edu
Download the NSSE's pocket guide for choosing a college.

Find Training

Should you go to college? I encourage you to consider going to college even if you choose an occupation that does not require the training. Earning an associate's or bachelor's degree can provide you with opportunities.

As you consider colleges, remember your goals. You are preparing for a particular occupation to help you be a person of influence.

Do not forget that going to college involves more than getting an education. College is an opportunity to grow and socialization is important as well. You will also be meeting people that will become a network, often friends for life.

Many of you will meet your spouse at college so for that reason I encourage you to strongly consider a Christian college. Doing so will also help you better prepare, especially if you will be going to graduate or professional school in the future.

Should you go to a big or small college? Often people choose a college for the wrong reason, like being a fan of the sports team or having friends who attend the college. You want to attend a college that will help you grow.

Many resources can help you as you choose. The College Navigator website can be used to compare colleges. Look at the class sizes at each school, the completion rate of programs, and the student to faculty ratio, which are important to your success.

Vocational Training

Suppose you are going the non-college route. A vocational education program (www.rvm.org) may work for you or perhaps enlisting in the military (www.todaysmilitary.com). If you are looking at a vocational school, examine the success rate (e.g., percentage to complete, percentage employed upon graduation) of the school. Make sure that the vocational school you are considering is licensed or accredited. You can find accredited schools at the U.S. Department of Education's website: www.ope.ed.gov/accreditation/. You can also find key information about the program you are interested in and compare them to other training programs as well.[35]

Going to School

Get to Know Your Advisor

If you go to school, make the most of it. In 2009, only 57.8 percent of students attending four-year colleges graduated in less than six years, and just 32.9 percent of those in two-year institutions graduated in three years. Perhaps this is why when people list their greatest regrets in life, education seems to be the biggest one.[36] So when you are thinking of getting slack and skipping a class, remember you are likely to regret that in 10 years (and even in 10 days when you have your mid-term). You can improve your chances of graduating in a timely manner by getting to know your advisor. In one study, talking to an academic advisor "sometimes" or "often" improved the chances of completion of both four-year and two-year students by as much as 53 percent.[37]

Meet with your advisor midway through each semester to select the classes you will take the next semester. Also, meet with him or her if you are having trouble of any kind—struggling with a class, considering dropping a class, and/or rethinking your major. Pay attention to the drop deadline for courses and consult with your advisor (and the course instructor) long before that deadline, especially if you are struggling.

> "If your knowledge doesn't cumulate, your troubles will." D. J. Foss

Adjust Well

Adjustment at college can be difficult. In one study, 54 percent of new students reported feeling isolated and lonely; 51 percent reported struggling with absence from family, and 45 percent reported struggling with absence from friends back home.

It is only natural to initially struggle with these kinds of feelings. If they persist, utilize your college counseling center. They can help you with these issues and others that may arise.

Other problems may be living situations in the dorm. Be proactive about dealing with these issues, not letting them grow into a major difficulty. Always try to deal with a situation calmly and objectively. Let the person know how his or her behavior affects you and others. State how you feel about the behavior, and always describe what can be done to fix things.[38]

Study Well

As you participate in your training, it is important to use your time well. You can get your training inexpensively if you are serious about your studies.

If you have conducted a serious personal assessment, there should be no need to jump from major to major. Remember some of you will be attending colleges where you have to apply for your major after attending two years. This major decision emphasizes the importance of starting well as soon as you arrive on campus. Find the library and spend a lot of time there. Find like-minded students who will challenge you and with whom you can study.

Preparing for Class

Try to get the syllabi for your classes before the course begins. Get your books (you might even begin reading them if you can) before the semester begins. Become familiar with your assignments. Develop a master calendar. Get the syllabi from each course and transfer the key dates (major projects due, papers, tests) onto one calendar. Develop a master schedule that will help you stay on track when a whim hits you. Put your sub-goals on a master calendar as well. Things will take longer than you think they will.[39]

Constantly set, achieve, and revise goals about your education and your future. Be very specific and keep track of your goals. For example, instead of setting a goal to make better history grades set a goal like I will spend 20% more time (or 3 more hours) studying this week to prepare for my history exam. Work hard at becoming the person God has made you to be and you will be on the road to becoming an influencer of the culture.

As you prepare to attend classes print out a map of the campus and locate the buildings where your classes will be held. Arrive to your class early. The only excuse for missing class is death and dying (of you or someone very close to you). The key to your success in class is being present, alert, and ready to learn. Sit in a place that maximizes your opportunity to stay alert. Note the rhythm of a class. Always remember, if you have only a few assignments, you have fewer opportunities to show what you know, the more important each one is.

Take notes. Actively process what you hear and make judgments about what to write down. Read the assigned material before you go to the lecture. Students who get down the supporting information benefit the most from note taking.[40] Listen for key phrases like, "the important point here is," "they key is," "as I've said before," and "remember." This is the material that is usually on the test![41]

Study

Actively review your notes, which is an important key to studying. The very act of taking a test is a learning experience, so start preparing for your exams on the first day of class. Studying good test performance leads to more studying.

Your study skills, habits, and attitudes are the top predictors of success over which you have control. What do you actually do when you study? The amount of time spent studying is not a good predictor of college grades. Be aware of your present knowledge state and know how far it is from the goal. Get active about getting from where you are to where you want to be. Genuine learning will occur when you study in a mindful way so frequently evaluate where you are.[42]

It would seem that the most effective way to study is to spend a massive amount of time on a subject. However, the research indicates that it is far more effective to spread the learning out over days. For example, five 2-hour sessions distributed over 5 days is superior to two 5-hour sessions concentrated in 2 days. Ten days of 1-hour sessions is better yet. You will do better if you spend a large amount of your time studying to be tested. This is called the retrieval effect. So give yourself frequent quizzes on the material you are studying. Test taking appears to improve learning in people of all ages.

However, you do need time for uninterrupted work so find blocks between classes. Find a quiet place to study and use it regularly. If you study in the same place all the time, you will recall the material better. If you are able to study in the classroom where the test will take place, that is even better. Do not multitask (surf the internet, respond to texts) when you are studying.[43]

Texting, social networking, and other media have been linked to poor academic performance, in a study of 483 female college freshmen across various forms of media: television, movies, music, surfing the Internet, social networking, talking on a cell phone, texting, reading magazines and newspapers, and playing video games. The participants reported their GPAs and academic confidence behaviors and problems. On average, the women spent nearly half their day engaged in some form of media use, particularly texting, listening to music, surfing the Internet, and social networking. Media use in general was associated with lower GPAs and other negative academic outcomes. On the other hand, newspaper reading and listening to music were linked to positive academic performance.[44]

As you study, read the text for your course. Try to understand the author's goals, and fig-

> **"There is no substitute for hard work."**
> **Thomas Edison**

ure out the main goal and sub-goals. It helps to preview a chapter before reading it. As you read, find the main points. Ask yourself questions about what you are reading (the retrieval affect). When you finish summarize what you have read. Get in the habit of reading to teach. Teach the material to a friend or classmate. The best way to learn is to teach.[45]

Know Where You Are

Get a handle on the environment you are in. Who is teaching your class? In academia, there are different

What do professors expect of you?[46]

Be a self-starter.
No excuses—even if you have a legitimate excuse.

classifications of instructors. These include instructor, assistant professor, associate professor, and (full) professor. Instructors tend to be professors who do not have a doctorate degree. Depending upon the college you are attending, this may be a person working on their doctorate degree and under the supervision of a professor. Assistant Professors tend to be professors who are fairly new. The key thing is that they lack tenure and have probably been teaching for less than seven years. Associate Professors tend to be teachers with some experience.

Put your best foot forward. Never use Mr. or Ms. always Dr. or Professor. By the way, the term doctor originally meant teacher.[47]

They probably have tenure. Full Professors (your syllabus will simply read Professor) have reached the highest rung of the academic echelon. They have tenure and seniority. They wield a great deal of power and responsibility. Why is all of this important? Let us suppose you are having trouble in a class taught by a Professor. Perhaps their teaching style is not to your liking. You complain to your advisor who is an

Assistant Professor. Professors make decisions about whether an Assistant Professor makes tenure and becomes Associate Professor. Do you get the picture? On the other hand, if your advisor is a Professor and an Assistant Professor teaches the course you are having trouble in, well then you might get somewhere. Hopefully, you will never have a need to complain about a situation but be aware of the structure. Should you have trouble with a course or your advisor, always go to them first. Treat each person with respect. If you continue to have difficulty, you can approach the Director of your program. This person will be acquainted with the entire faculty within the program and should be able to assist in working things out. If that fails, look toward the Department Chair. This person will be over all of the programs within a department. If that fails, go to the Dean of your School or College.

What should you be doing?

Look carefully then how you walk, not as unwise but as wise, making the best use of the time, because the days are evil. Therefore do not be foolish, but understand what the will of the Lord is.
Ephesians 5:15-17

Do not just mark time. Always think about what the key task for you is at a particular point in time and be looking at the next step to take. Donna Hembrick, the Director of Career Services at North Carolina Central University has identified some key tasks that students need to be accomplishing at particular stages of their training. During your freshmen year, invest in an interview suit or two, which will be needed later for job interviews and important functions. Consider doing a summer internship and getting involved in volunteer work. It is also a good idea to get involved in campus organizations that allow you the opportunity to develop leadership skills.

During your sophomore year, research at least three career options related to your major while pursuing leadership positions in campus organizations. Ask employers and professors to be prepared to write recommendations to future employers and graduate schools. Make good grades!

During your junior year, narrow down your career interests. Start developing your resume and cover letter. Take leadership positions in clubs and organizations, and ask employers and professors to write reference letters to employers and graduate schools. Complete at least five informational interviews, and shadow several professionals in your future field. Conduct research on potential employers. If graduate school or professional school is in your future, plan to take the Graduate Record Examinations (GRE), Law School Admission Test (LSAT), or Medical College Admission (MCAT) your junior year. Get some preparation materials and allow enough time to take these exams more than once so you can obtain the scores you need.

Keep track of your achievements to help you develop your resume

Work

School

Volunteer

Church

During your senior year participate in on-campus recruiting programs, and attend local association meetings

Check out the latest copy of R. N. Bolles' *What Color is Your Parachute?* Published by Ten Speed Press.

and network with potential employers. Engage in mock interviews for employment positions and graduate school. Read two or more professional or trade publications at least bi-weekly. If applicable,

Finding graduate schools:
www.Petersons.com

apply to graduate or professional schools. Attend career fairs. As you go through your training, develop a portfolio where you keep track of awards, special honors, experiences and training.[48]

You May Fail

It is important to realize you may fail. In research on performance we have learned that people who understand failure is a possibility are less likely to fail and perform better in school than those who do not think failure can happen.[49] Perhaps you are coming from an academic training program where people were passed along and not held back. College or vocational training will not be that way. You can expect to encounter great difficulty and you will need to work hard to succeed. How will you handle a situation when you encounter a setback like a bad grade?

How do you see yourself?

Some people encounter difficulty and begin to falter. They may see themselves as a failure. Should you find yourself struggling it will be important to engage in an activity called story editing. For example, in a situation where college students have performed poorly in their first year of study, those who have read articles about students who performed poorly initially, but improved over time tend to do so as well. This seemed especially to be the case when the students wrote out a narrative that described how they would do better once they learned the ropes. So if you struggle initially perhaps you might journal about how that is to be expected and that you will do better once you get your feet on the ground.[50] Don't you think Daniel, Hananiah, Mishael, and Azariah did something like that? Again, they were exiles of Judah; however, they must have seen themselves as prophets to the Babylonian kingdom or something else, which led to their success.

Preparing for the Next Steps

As you go through your training always think about the next step whether that is graduate school or a job. A few years ago, an interesting article was written for undergraduate psychology students on how to behave when attending a professional conference. Though it was intended for psychology students, you can adapt the information for your situation as well. The author noted when you find yourself in settings where there are potential employers (or professors who can admit you to graduate or professional school) create a people plan for the people you want to meet. This means you need to know something about their research or position. For optimal success, you might even email them ahead of time and ask if you may meet with them. When you do interact with them, ask good questions. Be very specific in your questioning of their research, college, or position. Do what you can to find a connection with them. It may be that they are from your state or share interest like your own. The authors emphasized being careful not to talk too much about yourself so you might briefly describe some research or work you have done but quickly relate it to the person you are speaking to. Do not be overly friendly or standoffish but try to strike the correct balance.[51]

Getting References

It is best to think now about references you will need in two or three years ahead of time. As you work on your class papers think about how you will need to ask that professor later for a reference. As you go to work, think about the kind of reference your supervisor will be making to future employers. As you conduct your training, you may do practicum and internships for which you will not be paid. Often students resist this not considering the vast responsibility and liability field supervisors undertake when they allow a student into their school or workplace. Always do your best and strive for excellence. These practicum and internship opportunities are the gateway to your

Requesting a Recommendation

Dr. Doe:

I took your class in the Fall of 2015 and received an A in the course. On my research paper you wrote, "This is an excellent specimen and thought provoking report." During the past year, I have taken 33 hours and earned a 3.8 GPA. I have attached my current resume as well as a description of the job/graduate school I am applying for/to. Please send the recommendations to _____ by January 15.

Thank you so much for your assistance.

Joe Doe

future. I got my first job after graduate school because my practicum supervisor knew the employer. Do your job well so that your professors and supervisors can write and make good recommendations for you. Help them write good letters for you by giving them information about the school or position you are applying to. Also, keep them up to date with your resume about your current activities. Though most recommendations are submitted electronically, if you are having a hard copy submitted, always provide the recommender with a self-addressed stamped envelope. If you are applying to graduate school, you will have the option to waive or not waive your right to see a recommendation. I often read recommendations where students have not waived their right to see it. I immediately negate the information contained therein. Why would you ask someone to recommend you and then not waive the right to review it? That informs me that the person does not trust the recommender. So perform with excellence so that you can be confident people will write good recommendations for you.

Preparing for the Interview

Always go to interviews prepared. This means you need to know all you can about the interviewer and their organization. If the interview is dealing with a graduate or professional school, know the kind of research the faculty have conducted and examine books they have written. You can find this information by googling their name and looking for their curriculum vita. You may be able to find a resume of employers who might interview you. Examine as much information about the school you are applying to or the company, church, or organization in which you are trying to get employment. Always make sure your clothes are clean and pressed well before the interview. At the interview, be prepared to take notes, and have copies of your resume ready. It is wise to be at least 20 minutes early to the interview and know that you may be taken early if the interviewer is ahead of time. As you approach the site of the interview, walk briskly and smile. You may be watched because interviewers often believe they can learn more by observation. You should never chew gum when you may be observed. During the interview, stick to facts and avoid showing strong feelings like extreme happiness or anger. After the interview, identify what went well and what did not go so well in the interview and strive to improve. It is a nice touch to send a thank you note to the interviewer.[52]

Into the Workforce

> Bondservants, obey in everything those who are your earthly masters, not by way of eye-service, as people-pleasers, but with sincerity of heart, fearing the Lord. Whatever you do, <u>work heartily, as for the Lord</u> and not for men, knowing that from the Lord you will receive the inheritance as you reward. You are serving the Lord Christ. For the wrongdoer will

> be paid back for the wrong he has done,
> and there is no partialilty.
> Colossians 3:22-25

As you go into the workforce set yourself apart by doing well. According to State of the American Workplace, a new report by Gallup Inc., only 30 percent of the U.S. workforce is engaged in their work. The remaining 70 percent of American workers are non-engaged or actively disengaged. This takes a toll and is believed to cost between $450 billion and $550 billion a year to U.S. companies.[53]

Unfortunately, meaningful work is not the norm. But if you are doing what you love to do and working as if you are doing it for the Lord you will excel. I suspect if you went back to the time of Daniel and picked up an article called Babylonian Workplace you would have learned that only 30 percent of the Babylonian workforce was engaged in their work. The remaining 70 percent were non-engaged or actively disengaged at a great cost to the Babylonian kingdom. Daniel, Hananiah, Mishael, and Azariah were engaged and they excelled because they realized God had prepared them for the tasks they were called upon to perform in Babylon. This led them to be engaged in their work and influence their culture. You too can be a influence if you be what God made you to be.

Chapter 4

Be An Investor

Into the Community

*Build houses and live in them; plant gardens and
eat their produce. Take wives and have sons and
daughters; take wives for your sons, and give your
daughters in marriage, that they may bear sons and
daughters; multiply there, and do not decrease. But
seek the welfare of the city where I have sent you
into exile, and pray to the Lord on its behalf, for in its
welfare you will find your welfare.*
Jeremiah 29:5-7

Jeremiah instructed Judah to build homes, families, and relationships when they were exiled. Though you may not be a prisoner in another land, you can learn from their model. To influence the community you must go into it and build relationships. This will require an investment into people.

Daniel was an investor in people. When God gave him the answer to Nebuchadnezzar's dream, Nebuchadnezzar promoted Daniel. Daniel did not forget his friends. Daniel used his position to bring

Hananiah, Mishael, and Azariah along with him. Daniel 2:49 says, "Daniel made a request of the king, and he appointed Shadrach, Meshach, and Abednego over the affairs of the province of Babylon. But Daniel remained at the king's court."

Barnabas: A Model Investor in Others

Encourager
Thus Joseph, who was also called by the apostles Barnabas (which means son of encouragement), a Levite, a native of Cyprus, sold a field that belonged to him and brought the money and laid it at the apostles' feet.
Acts 4:36-37

Connector
And when he had come to Jerusalem, he attempted to join the disciples. And they were all afraid of him, for they did not believe that he was a disciple. But Barnabas took him and brought him to the apostles and declared to them how on the road he had seen the Lord, who spoke to him, and how at Damascus he had preached boldly in the name of Jesus.
Acts 9:26-27

Elevator
While they were worshiping the Lord and fasting, the Holy Spirit said, "Set apart for me Barnabas and Saul for the work to which I have called them."
Acts 13:2

And after the meeting of the synagogue broke up, many Jews and devout converts to Judaism followed Paul and Barnabas, who, as they spoke with them, urged them to continue in the grace of God.
Acts 13:43

We see another example of a man who invested in others in the New Testament when we read about a man named Barnabas. We meet Barnabas in Acts 4:36-37 as he is giving a sizable contribution to the early church. His name had been changed from Joseph to Barnabas, which meant encouragement. He must have had a knack for lifting others up. Next, we find him ministering to Saul who would later become known as Paul in Acts 9:26-27. Saul had become a Christian but most of the Christians were afraid of him. Barnabas courageously took Paul and brought him to the apostles. Barnabas saw someone who had potential when he looked at Paul. He nurtured and mentored Paul as you may a new student or employee one day. In Acts 11:25, we see that Barnabas went to Tarsus to find Paul and bring him to Antioch where they taught together and took famine relief funds to Judea (Acts 11:30). Barnabas spent time with Paul, and he as well as the entire church benefited from it.

Often we fail to invest in others because of jealousy, fear of getting proper credit, or concern that the one we are helping may surpass us. Barnabas was more concerned about advancing the kingdom than himself. In Acts

A Risky Investment

And a young man followed him, with nothing but a linen cloth about his body. And they seized him, but he left the linen cloth and ran away naked.
Mark 14:51-52

Now Paul and his companions set sail from Paphos and came to Perga in Pamphylia. And John left them and returned to Jerusalem.
Acts 13:13

That reaped dividends

Aristarchus my fellow prisoner greets you, and Mark the cousin of Barnabas (concerning whom you have received instructions—if he comes to you, welcome him).
Colossians 4:10

Luke alone is with me. Get Mark and bring him with you, for he is very useful to me for ministry.
2 Timothy 4:11

She who is at Babylon, who is likewise chosen, sends you greetings, and so does Mark, my son.
1 Peter 5:13

13, we see a shift in importance when the names of Paul and Barnabas are reversed. By Acts 14 Paul is being referred to as the chief speaker and appears to be more important than Barnabas.

Rather than becoming jealous, Barnabas was probably thrilled to see God working through him to develop Paul into a great leader.

Later Barnabas made a risky investment in a young man named John Mark? Who was John Mark? In the Gospel of Mark we learn that there was a man who was following Jesus as He was about to be crucified. After some young men tried to grab him he ran away naked (Mark 14:51-52). Since Mark's gospel is the only gospel to mention this incident, many conclude the young man was Mark. If this were the case, he probably had a lot to overcome and many questioned the wisdom of Barnabas and Paul in taking him on a grueling missionary journey. The book of Acts indicates that John Mark abandoned the missionary journey (Acts 15:38), which probably led many people to say to Barnabas and Paul, "I told you so." However, when Paul suggested that he and Barnabas return on a missionary journey, trouble arose as Barnabas suggested they take John Mark with them. In Acts 15, we read this lead to a great conflict between Barnabas and Paul, and they eventually separated with Paul taking Silas and Barnabas taking John Mark on a separate journey. This had to be difficult for Barnabas as his relationship with Paul was strained. Barnabas' investment in John Mark paid dividends.

Ten years later Paul described John Mark as profitable, a fellow worker, and someone he would like to see (Colossians 4:10, Philemon 24; 2 Timothy 4:11). Others also saw the value of John Mark. Peter referred to John Mark as his son (1 Peter 5:13). John Mark wrote the gospel of Mark, which many have characterized as the memoirs of Peter. He is believed to have visited Egypt and founded the church at Alexandria. Many believe as recorded in Fox's Book of Martyrs that he was dragged through the streets of Alexandria and killed before their idol, Serapis. John Mark became a man who would not run away or quit even when his life was threatened.

Investing in Others is an Investment in Yourself

Investing in others is about being in relationship with other people. Relationships are out of vogue these days. Research indicates that people have fewer friends and acquaintances than in the past.[54] Yet, we need friends. Somewhere, either in Judah before the collapse of their country, perhaps on the road to Babylon or after arriving in Babylon, Daniel, Hananiah, Mishael, and Azariah found each other. This helped them to become influencers of the culture rather than being influenced by it. We know from research that people become wise when they associate with wise people and foolish when they associate with foolish people. In a recent study, high school students were asked to categorize their peers as best friends, friends, acquaintances, strangers, or relatives. The researchers then mapped out how students performed in school relative to their peer group. The results indicated that students who associated with other students who performed well academically were themselves more likely to perform well academically. If their grades improved their friend's grades improved. The opposite was also true. When a student's GPA dropped, the GPAs of their peers dropped as well.[55] We become like the people we associate with so choose your associates carefully.

I love reading and watching The Lord of the Rings by J. R. R. Tolkien, and The Chronicles of Narnia by C. S. Lewis. It seems obvious these men had an influence upon one another. For many years C. S. Lewis, J. R. R. Tolkien, Charles Williams, and their friends spent time with one another. Their group of friends became known as "The Inklings." Based on a perusal of the bookshelves of my local bookstore (and a review of top movies over the past years) it appears they continue to influence the culture today. Does this kind of thing happen to people like us?

At Welch College (formerly Free Will Baptist Bible College) a quartet called the Gospeliers formed around the Fall of 1950. At some point, the quartet consisted of Robert Picirilli, Bobby Jackson,

For Dr. Picirilli and Bobby Jackson on Welch quartet at survivingculture.com
James Earl Raper, and Eugene Waddell. They travelled for the college to recruit students and raise funds as they made their way through school. They continued to do so even after graduating. All four went on to graduate school in South Carolina colleges while continuing to travel for Welch College. They went on to become very successful ministers. Picirilli earned a Ph.D. and returned to Welch College as a professor, and eventually became the Academic Dean. He also served as the moderator of the National Association of Free Will Baptists. Bobby Jackson became the most well-known and traveled evangelist of the Free Will Baptist denomination, and he too served as the moderator of the National Association of Free Will Baptists. James Earl Raper pastored for decades and served as a trustee for Welch College, and headed a children's home in east Tennessee. Eugene Waddell became a pastor and later the director of Free Will Baptist International Missions. Do you think they had an impact upon one another?

Among these were Daniel, Mishael,
and Azariah of the tribe of Judah.
Daniel 1:6

I suspect if you think about your own life you will already find evidence of this principle. If you had approached me during my senior year of high school and asked me to name my best friends, I suspect I would have said, "Ronald Suggs and Jerry Jarman." Interestingly, all three of us went on to earn doctorate degrees of some kind. At a recent reunion, I learned that most of our classmates have gone on and become involved in a local church. Proverbs 13:20 teaches us that "Whoever walks with the wise becomes wise, but the companion of fools will suffer harm." I can certainly say that has been true in my life. If you want to become wise, hang around wise people.

Daniel, Hananiah, Mishael, and Azariah were companions. The book of 2 Kings tells us thousands of people were exiled from Judah so there were many others with which they could have associated with. What made them decide to build relationships with one another?

> ...they sought Daniel and his companions, to kill them....Then Daniel went to his house and made the matter known to Hananiah, Mishael, and Azariah, his companions, and told them to seek mercy from the God of heaven concerning this mystery, so that Daniel and his companions might not be destroyed with the rest of the wise men of Babylon.
> Daniel 2:13, 17-18

What do you look for in companions?

Look for Exiles

Arioch referred to Daniel as an exile (Daniel 2:25). Even after experiencing great success, the wicked King Belshazzar called Daniel an exile (Daniel 5:13). When the jealous officials tried to entrap Daniel, they referred to him as an exile (Daniel 6:13). Though Daniel, Hananiah, Mishael, and Azariah had great aptitude, and became very successful the Babylonians always thought of them differently. An exile is someone who is out of place. They do not quite fit in because their home is elsewhere. The writer of Hebrews refers to all believers as exiles.

> "Daniel, who is <u>one of the exiles from Judah,</u> pays no attention to you, O king..."
> Daniel 6:13

Look for people who are more interested in doing what is right than fitting in. There will always be those who adopt the ways of the corrupt culture as a means to fit in, an exile like these four is comfortable being an outsider. They also love the Lord more than the world. To be an exile is to be in good company. Moses became an exile when he chose God over the riches of Egypt.

Exiles

"I have found among the __exiles__ from Judah..."
Daniel 2:25

"...You are that Daniel, one of the __exiles of Judah__, whom the king my father brought from Judah."
Daniel 5:13

...Moses fled and became an __exile__....
Acts 7:29

These all died in faith... and having acknowledged that they were strangers and __exiles on the earth__.
Hebrews 11:13

In addition to seeking exiles, it is important to seek those who will help us develop into the people God has planned for us to be.

How does one find a community of "exiles?"
Ask...

Are they comfortable in their own skin?

Is God or other things their top priority?

Do not love the world or the things in the world. If anyone loves the world, the love of the Father is not in him.
1 John 2:15

> *Competent to stand in the king's palace,*
> *and to teach them the literature and*
> *language of the Chaldeans.*
> *Daniel 1:4b*

Look for Learners

Daniel, Hananiah, Mishael, and Azariah had a desire to learn. Find places and associate with people where learning is valued. Avoid those who model (and teach) that which is wrong, or are satisfied with mediocrity.

> *Give instruction to a wise man, and he will*
> *be still wiser; teach a righteous man,*
> *and he will increase in learning.*
> *Proverbs 9:9*

When I was in college, I worked at a luxury condominium to help pay my way through school. The residents encouraged us to learn by providing us with newspapers like the Wall Street Journal. In addition, they frequently provided us with educational magazines and books as well as occasional tickets to hear the Nashville Symphony. The workplace seemed to attract people who wanted to learn. Among the group, most went on to earn graduate degrees. The occupations obtained by the workers includes Pastors, University Professors, a College President, an Air Force Chaplain, school teachers, and a publishing company Vice President. Frequent topics for discussion among the workers were how to get into a good graduate school, as well as discussions about music, history, and current events. Though we were from different backgrounds and regions of the country, we all wanted to learn. I learned that in this type of community, competence and a love for learning become contagious.

> Then _Daniel replied with prudence_ and discretion
> to Arioch, the captain of the king's guard, who had
> gone out to kill the wise men of Babylon.
> Daniel 2:14

Look for Prudence

Characteristics of the Prudent

In everything _the prudent acts with knowledge_.
Proverbs 13:16a

One who is wise is _cautious_ and turns away from evil.
Proverbs 14:16a

The _prudent_ sees danger and hides himself.
Proverbs 22:3a

It is an honor for a man to keep aloof from strife.
Proverbs 20:3a

Prudence is the ability to know how to act, to behave mannerly. Daniel was a model in prudence. He demonstrated prudence with the eunuch, Arioch, and Nebuchadnezzar. Spend time with people who are prudent. It is found among those who do their best to avoid evil. They see when danger is present and a situation needs to be avoided. Prudent people do not waste time arguing over trivial matters.

> And over them three high officials, of whom Daniel
> was one, to whom these satraps should give ac-
> count, so the king might suffer no loss.
> Daniel 6:2

Look for Diligence

The diligence of Daniel led him to ascend as an administrator. Look for diligent people. Diligence is similar to prudence. Diligent people are those who work hard and are focused on getting things done. Diligent people can be entrusted with a task and you can know it will be done. In a community of diligent people there tends to be an atmosphere where work and achievement are the expectation. Our culture is drifting away from diligence. Today 1 in 7 people between the ages of 16 and 24 in the top 25 major U. S. cities are not in school or working. Diligent people are increasingly in the minority. However, the diligent are likely to grow in popularity just as Daniel, Hananiah, Mishael, and Azariah did. It is estimated that those 1 out of 7 people (5.8 million youth) cost $93.7 billion dollars in government support and in lost revenue every year.[56]

> **Characteristics of the Diligent**
>
> The hand of the _diligent_ makes rich.
> He who gathers in summer is a prudent son.
> Proverbs 10:4b, 5a
>
> In all toil there is profit.
> Proverbs 14:23a
>
> Whoever works his land will have plenty of bread.
> Proverbs 12:11a

And the king spoke with them, and among all of them none was found like Daniel, Hananiah, Mishael, and Azariah. Therefore they stood before the king.
Daniel 1:19

How do you find them? Thin Slicing

How do you know if someone possesses these traits? You can find the people you need to be with if you learn to analyze thin slices. Thin slicing is the ability to make a quick determination based on a brief interaction. If you think about it, you can identify quickly those who are good for you. Watch what people do. Pay more attention to what they do rather than what they say.

Thin Slicing by...	Method	Looking for...
Nebuchadnezzar	Questioning	Competence
Abraham's servant	Observation	Care for Others
Jethro	Inquiry	Courage

For example, college students are very skilled at thin slicing. Most college students can watch a short video of a professor and correctly predict if that pro-

> Rev. David Paramore on studying people at survivingculture.com

fessor is effective. Students ratings after viewing a short video of a professor teaching have been found to match the student ratings of instruction the professor receives from students who spend an entire semester with him or her.[57] Physicians can easily look at the vital signs of a patient and quickly determine if their life is in danger. I experienced thin slicing (and have since utilized it) when interviewing for graduate schools.

Nebuchadnezzar used thin slicing when he interviewed Daniel, Hananiah, Mishael and Azariah by the kinds of questions he asked, he was able to determine they were ten times better than the other youth. Abraham's servant used thin slicing to find a wife for Isaac. He prayed that the one who gave him water would be the one (Genesis 24). Moses' father-in-law used thin slicing (before he was Moses' father-in-law) to get Moses into the family. His daughters told him a man had defended them when they were trying to get water for their flock (Exodus 2:19-20). Jethro's response was, "And where is he? Which meant, "Get him; we can use a man like that around here." Some employers use thin slicing when they take an applicant out for dinner and watch how they treat wait staff. Get into the habit of studying people by utilizing thin slicing. Watch how people you interact with treat someone they have power and/or position over, perhaps doubting the person can do anything for them.

> When she had finished giving him a drink, she said,
> "I will draw water for your camels also, until they
> have finished drinking." So she quickly emptied her
> jar into the trough and ran again to the well to draw
> water, and she drew for all his camels. *The man
> gazed at her in silence to learn whether the Lord had
> prospered his journey or not.*
> Genesis 24:19-21

> They said, *"An Egyptian delivered us out of the hand
> of the shepherds and even drew water for us and
> watered the flock."* He said to his daughters, "Then
> where is he? Why have you left the man? Call him,
> that he may eat bread."
> Exodus 2:19-20

Proverbs on Those to Avoid

<u>Characteristic</u>	<u>Proverb</u>
The unprepared	*A <u>slack</u> hand causes poverty.. He who <u>sleeps in</u> <u>harvest</u> is a son who brings <u>shame</u>.* Proverbs 10:4a, 5b
The undependable	*Like vinegar to the teeth and smoke to the eyes, so is the <u>sluggard</u> to those who send him.* Proverbs 10:26
The excuse maker	*The sluggard says, "<u>There is a lion outside</u>! I shall be killed in the streets!"* Proverbs 22:13
The time waster	*He who follows worthless pursuits lacks sense.* Proverbs 12:11b
Those who engage in dangerous behavior	*The prudent sees danger and hides himself, but <u>the simple go on and suffer for it</u>.* Proverbs 22:3
The Talker	*Mere talk tends only to poverty.* Proverbs 14:23b
The Opinionated	*A fool takes no pleasure in understanding, but only in expressing his opinion.* Proverbs 18:2

If someone has negative characteristics like those described in the Proverbs, ask yourself, "Who is influencing whom?" "Am I becoming more like them or am I influencing them away from these traits?" To influence the culture, you must quickly determine who can help you grow, whom you can help grow, and who you should avoid lest they derail you from growing.

Let each of you look not only to his own interests,
but also to the interests of others.
Philippians 2:4

Givers, Takers, and Matchers

Dr. Adam Grant is an Organizational Psychologist who has extensively studied workplace behavior trying to determine who succeeds and who fails. In his book, *Give and Take*, he describes three categories of workers: givers, takers, and matchers. Givers are those who enjoy helping others and will do so with no strings attached, like the Philippians 2 admonition to put the needs of others before yourself. Takers are those who are trying to get as much as they can from people while only giving back what they must. Matchers try to maintain an even balance of give and take. After examining Dr. Grant's research, it appears that his definition of a giver is consistent with the kind of person we are admonished to be in the Scripture. For example, the Good Samaritan is a model for this kind of giving. It also seems consistent with the approach Daniel took as he dealt with others. When Daniel was promoted after finding the answer to King Nebuchadnezzar's dream, he also requested that Hananiah, Mishael, and Azariah be promoted.

*Daniel made a request of the king,
and he appointed Shadrach, Meshach,
and Abednego over the affairs of the province of
Babylon. But Daniel remained at the king's court.
Daniel 2:49*

We can also see Daniel's behavior as a giver when we look at his work with Nebuchadnezzar and Belshazzar. He tried to help Nebuchadnezzar just before he lost his mind for a period of years, and Belshazzar just before he was overthrown and killed. In Scripture we are called to give, you might say it is a key to the "good life." You would think givers would succeed. When you look at the data, givers sink to the bottom of the success ladder whether you are looking at engineers, salespeople, or physicians. However, givers are also at that top of the success ladder. In the occupations Grant has examined, givers have been at the bottom and the top of the success ladder. How can this be explained? Grant calls the unsuccessful givers selfless givers. They give to others, drop their goals, and give without thinking of the impact. Successful givers are careful to examine whom they will help and how much they will help them. Successful givers tend to help other givers or matchers rather than takers. The research indicates it is dangerous to help takers because they will take advantage of you.[58] At first I was bothered by this until I began to realize this is consistent with Scripture.

In all things I have shown you that by working hard in this way we must help the weak and remember the words of the Lord Jesus, how he himself said, "It is more blessed to give than to receive."
Acts 20:35

Give to Givers

Jesus did not blindly invest in everyone. As you examine His life, you see much of it was concentrated on 12 rather than 24 or 36 people. Eleven of the 12 appear to have been givers as exhibited in their selfless sharing of the gospel as seen in Acts 2. Jesus invested in people who were (or became) givers, He instructed us to move to another when our giving is not received. He said in Matthew 10:14, "And if anyone will not receive you or listen to your words, shake off the dust from your feet when you leave that house or town."

Faithful are the wounds of a friend;
profuse are the kisses of an enemy.
Proverbs 27:6

Proverbs 27:17 tells us that as "Iron sharpens iron, one man sharpens another" indicating there can be some friction as we help one another develop. Sometimes development will involve reproof ("Reprove a wise man, and he will love you" Proverbs 9:8b), letting someone know when they have done something wrong or when there is a better way of doing things. Therefore, the giving and receiving of reproof will be a key element to help us determine if we should continue to give of ourselves to a particular person. How do we know if we are dealing with a taker? Throughout Proverbs, there are three types of problematic people that are mentioned: the simple, scoffers, and fools.

> How long, O <u>simple</u> ones, will you love being sim-
> ple? How long will <u>scoffers</u> delight in their
> scoffing and <u>fools</u> hate knowledge?
> Proverbs 1:22

Avoid Scoffers

The Proverbs teach us to avoid the scoffer. What is a scoffer? The scoffer is a person who hates truth and ridicules those who try to correct them. Scoffers are often cynical and bitter. We run the risk of being influenced by them if we remain with them, which is one reason you are told to avoid them. How do you know you cannot help them? Consider Jesus' model for confrontation in Matthew 18 when dealing with the scoffer. There comes a time when it is obvious a person will not listen to us and at that point, it becomes an issue of being a good steward of the amount of time you have. Avoid the scoffer so they cannot influence you, so that you may invest your time in efforts that are more productive. Isolating the scoffer might actually give them the opportunity to see their error and cease scoffing.

How do you know?	
Hatred for correction	*But he who hates reproof is stupid.* Proverbs 12:1b
	A scoffer does not like to be reproved; he will not go to the wise. Proverbs 15:12
Attacks helper	*Whoever corrects a scoffer gets himself abuse, and he who reproves a wicked man incurs injury. Do not reprove a scoffer, or he will hate you.* Proverbs 9:7-8a

Avoid Fools

A second group of people we are told to avoid are fools. The foolish are dangerous. They do things that waste time, and inflict harm. They drag people down and can do much damage. You can try to help them with correction as we are instructed to provide in Proverbs 26:5, "Answer a fool according to his folly, lest he be wise in his own eyes."

If they respond you can be a positive influence in their life. If they fail to respond positively it will become time to move on, as Proverbs 26:4 indicates, "Answer not a fool according to his folly, lest you be like him yourself."

How do you know?	
Despise instruction	*Fools despise wisdom and instruction.* Proverbs 1:7b
Proud of being stupid	*In everything the prudent acts with knowledge, but a fool flaunts his folly.* Proverbs 13:16
Bad influence	*Leave the presence of a fool, for there you do not meet words of knowledge.* Proverbs 14:7

Dangerous	*Whoever ignores instruction despises himself. Proverbs 15:32a*
	Let a man meet a she-bear robbed of her cubs rather than a fool in his folly. Proverbs 17:12
	A fool is reckless and careless. Proverbs 14:16b

There is a clear difference between those we are to avoid and those we are called upon to embrace.

Proverbs on Those to Embrace

Trait	Proverb
Careful	*The prudent gives thought to his steps. Proverbs 14:15b*
Confidant	*A man of understanding remains silent. Proverbs 11:12b*
Truth teller	*Righteous lips are the delight of a king, and he loves him who speaks what is right. Proverbs 16:13*
Humble	*Humility comes before honor. Proverbs 15:33b*
Generous	*He who is generous to the needy honors him. Proverbs 14:31b*

Build Relationships

In 1985, the typical person had three people with whom they could confide important information. Twenty years later in 2004, the typical person indicated they had zero people with whom they could confide. This is very sad.[59] A researcher challenged these findings which led to a reexamination of the data. The results supported the earlier findings and further indicated that a gap in relationships is often concealed by the prevalence of social networks. In other words, people have fewer and fewer friends today, though a larger number of friends on Facebook or followers on Twitter often conceal this problem. In fact, the number of close friends and confidants has actually decreased since the arrival of social media.[60] Truly, you will be an outlier should you engage in building relationships.

Be Friendly

A man that hath friends must shew himself friendly:
and there is a friend that sticketh closer than a brother.
Proverbs 18:24 KJV

To begin to build relationships be intentional about being friendly and spending quality time with those you target. Start by really being with people. This means there will be times when you put the cell phone and other media aside. We know from research that the mere presence of a cell phone on a table reduces in-person conversation quality. In one study, researchers placed a mobile phone of the participants on a table between them. They were compared to a group who placed a spiral notebook between them and a peer. The results indicated that the presence of the cell phone negatively affected closeness, connection, and conversation quality.[61] To be friendly, be with whomever you are with rather than being focused on texting or other media.

Be Kind

Bear with others realizing they are not perfect as you are not perfect so be willing to give them the benefit of doubt. Go out of your way to be kind to others and forgive them of their imperfections. It also helps to put Ephesians 4:32 into practice, "Be kind to one another, tenderhearted, forgiving one another, as God in Christ forgave you."

Be a Confidant

Establish yourself as trustworthy, Proverbs 11:13 says, "He who is trustworthy in spirit keeps a thing covered." Be a person that can be entrusted to maintain the confidence of others. Do not repeat what other people tell you. Be alert for the gossip kings and queens who fish for information about others. Develop a habit of talking to people rather than about other people.

Be There

> Two are better than one, because they have a good reward for their toil. For if they fall, one will lift up his fellow. But woe to him who is alone when he falls and has not another to lift him up! Again, if two lie together, they keep warm, but how can one keep warm alone? And though a man might prevail against one who is alone, two will withstand him—a threefold cord is not quickly broken.
> Ecclesiastes 4:9-12

Proverbs 17:17 says, "A friend loves at all times, and a brother is born for adversity." Be there for your friends in the good times and the bad.

Work on creating the warmth relationship described in Ecclesiastes 4:11. Also, work on being there for your friend as they encounter difficulty. Real relationships are built when we help our friends in their time of need. When your friends encounter difficulties, be they school or work problems, relationship problems, or health problems make sure you are there for them. The opposite is also true. When you encounter difficulties note those who are around you at that time. They are the real deal.

Be a Mentor

Invest in someone. Find someone who is not as far along as you. Perhaps they are younger or new to a place where you are. A good model for this kind of investment is that which Barnabas gave to Paul after he became a believer.

What is mentoring?

Characteristic	Titus 2
A willingness to be different	1 But as for you, teach what accords with sound doctrine.
Showing people how to live	2 Older men are to be sober-minded, dignified, self-controlled, sound in faith, in love, and in steadfastness. 3 Older women likewise are to be reverent in behavior, not slanderers or slaves to much wine. They are to teach what is good,... 7 Show yourself in all respects to be a model of good works, and in your teaching show integrity, dignity, 8 and sound speech that cannot be condemned,
Training	4 and so train...5 to be self-controlled, pure, working...6 Likewise, urge the younger men to be self-controlled.
Practical	9...be submissive to their own masters in everything; they are to be well-pleasing, not argumentative, 10 not pilfering, but showing all good faith, so that in everything they may adorn the doctrine of God our Savior.
	12 training us to renounce ungodliness and worldly passions, and to live self-controlled, upright, and godly lives in the present age,...15 Declare these things; exhort and rebuke with all authority. Let no one disregard you.
Why mentor?	5...that the word of God may not be reviled. 8...so that an opponent may be put to shame, having nothing evil to say about us.

Find a Mentor

Make sure you too find a mentor. Look for them among your professors, supervisors, older students, and more experienced employees. A good place to find mentors is in a local church.

Find a Church

Wherever you go, you will always need to be part of a family of believers. The Bible teaches us that a Christian without a church community is vulnerable. God uses the church to impact the world, so find a church and get involved. Resist the temptation to church shop or become a critic of churches. Find a body of believers, unite with them in spite of their imperfections, and immerse yourself into the body. Note, there are no perfect churches so do not run at the first sign of dif-

Pray We

Then I turned my face to the Lord God, seeking him by prayer and pleas for mercy with fasting and sackcloth and ashes.
Daniel 9:3

I prayed to the LORD my God and made confession, saying, "O Lord, the great and awesome God, who keeps covenant and steadfast love with those who love him and keep his commandments, we have sinned and done wrong and acted wickedly and rebelled, turning aside from your commandments and rules.
Daniel 9:4-5

We have not listened to your servants the prophets, who spoke in your name to our kings, our princes, and our fathers, and to all the people of the land.
Daniel 9:6

ficulty. Someone has described a church as a group of porcupines on a winter night. They seriously need to get close to one another for warmth but are constantly pricking one another. Today the tendency is for one to become upset with people at a church and then move on to the next one. This robs one of their ability to mature and develop. Get in the habit of seeing yourself as part of the church and responsible for its success. Note the way Daniel saw himself and prayed for the people of Judah (Daniel 9). Had Daniel committed egregious sins? Probably not—but he constantly prayed "I" and "we." He identified with Judah and accepted responsibility for their action. He considered himself a participant rather than a spectator.

What do you look for in a church community? Look for a place where you will be challenged to grow in the Word. Look for people who will be good models for you to learn how to live. Look for a place to get involved and use your gifts, and remember there are no perfect churches.

When I was in college I had a privilege of playing (mostly I just practiced with the team) on the first basketball team at Welch College. Previously most of us had been on various society sports teams where we competed against each other. To address some of this our coach implemented an exercise where we would end practice every morning with a teammate shooting free throws. If the teammate made both free throws, practice was over. But if they missed we had to run what was called suicides (a well named exercise). We then returned to the baseline and another teammate would shoot again. If they missed, we ran again. As a result, this group of rivals quickly meshed into what became a real team. It did not matter who was at the free throw line, it felt like we all were there. Choose your community carefully but once you choose, think and pray "we." Stick it out in the good times as well as the bad and you and that community will grow.

Interaction in the Community

How should you interact in the community? According to Titus 2 it is wise to find older people in your church and other settings and to get to know them. It can be hard to interact with people who are so different from you but the Scripture will help. We are told in 1 Timothy 5:1, "Do not rebuke an older man." Rebuking an older man can be a real relationship killer! The passage goes on to say instead "encourage him as you would a father." So treat older people as you would like people to treat your parents or grandparents. Try to seek out the older people in your church and minister to them by visiting with them. Ask them questions about their life, and take advantage of these opportunities. Remember, you are helping yourself as well as the person you are with. Ask the older person for advice. Do not miss an opportunity to interview and learn from an older person.

> ### Get to know an older couple at your church
> ### Questions to ask:
>
> How did you meet your spouse?
>
> What was it like when you were growing up?
>
> What advice do you have for me as I grow?

The Scripture also teaches us how to treat same age peers as siblings (1 Timothy 5:2). You are probably recognizing a theme; the community of the church is a family where we help one another as we walk with the Lord.

"Behold, the days are coming, when all that is in your house, and that which your fathers have stored up till this day, shall be carried to Babylon. Nothing shall be left, says the LORD. And some of your own sons, who will come from you, whom you will father, shall be taken away, and they shall be eunuchs in the palace of the king of Babylon."
Isaiah 39:6-7

To Marry or Not to Mary

Now as a concession, not a command,
I say this. I wish that all were as I myself am.
But each has his own gift from God,
one of one kind and one of another.
1 Corinthians 7:6-7

As you read the book of Daniel there is no mention of Daniel, Hananiah, Mishael, or Azariah having a wife. One hundred years before the fall of Jerusalem, King Hezekiah attempted to gain favor from the Babylonians by showing them his treasures. He was being disobedient to God and he was depending upon the Babylonians to protect him (rather than God) from Assyria. The prophecy in Isaiah 39:7 indicates that many of the royal family will become eunuchs and serve in the palace of the king of Babylon. Therefore, it is very possible that Daniel, Hananiah, Mishael, and Azariah may have been eunuchs. If this were the case, clearly a single person can influence the culture. We see further evidence of this when Paul admonished those who can be single to consider it a gift and a way to serve the Lord unencumbered (1 Corinthians 7:7). You will have to make your own determination about whether God has called you to be single.

Finding a Spouse

An excellent wife who can find?
She is far more precious than jewels.
Proverbs 31:10

Should you choose to be single, do so for the right reasons. There is an alarming trend in our culture where many are turned off by the idea of marriage so if you are married or get married, you will be in the minority in the United States.[62] Many are cohabitating, engaging in the sexual hook up culture but are not interested in building a family or being a spouse. After deciding to follow Christ, the most important decision you will make is if you should get married and if so to whom. The same strategies previously described like thin slicing can help you to identify a spouse.

In fact, Dr. John Gottman, a psychologist with decades of experience has conducted extensive research on marital relationships.

Thin Slicing on What to Avoid

Nonbelievers	Do not be unequally yoked with unbelievers. For what partnership has righteousness with lawlessness? Or what fellowship has light with darkness? 2 Corinthians 6:14
Criticism	But now you must put them all away: anger, wrath, malice, slander, and obscene talk from your mouth. Colossians 3:8
	Let no corrupting talk come out of your mouths, but only such as is good for building up, as fits the occasion, that it may give grace to those who hear. Ephesians 4:29
Contempt	But if you bite and devour one another, watch out that you are not consumed by one another. Galatians 5:15
Defensiveness	Therefore, confess your sins to one another and pray for one another, that you may be healed. The prayer of a righteous person has great power as it is working. James 5:16
Stonewalling	Be angry and do not sin; do not let the sun go down on your anger. Ephesians 4:26

Gottman has been able to look at couples before they are married and predict with 94 percent accuracy who will stay together. He identified four key characteristics that are toxic to the marital relationship: criticism, contempt, stonewalling, and defensiveness.[63] You can use thin slicing by looking for these characteristics to determine if you are in a healthy relationship. The best predictor of future behavior is past behavior. If you find yourself being treated with contempt or a lot of criticism, you are in an unhealthy relationship. Whatever you see in a dating relationship will likely be magnified many times over should you marry the person.

How can you know what someone is like? Again, look at thin slicing. Abraham's servant knew he had a good prospect in Rebecca when she willingly provided water for him and his camels (Genesis 24). She was caring and industrious. You too must be on the lookout for someone of virtue.

> **Go beyond looks**
>
> *Like a gold ring in a pig's snout is a beautiful woman without discretion.*
> Proverbs 11:22
>
> *An excellent wife is the crown of her husband, but she who brings shame is like rottenness in his bones.*
> Proverbs 12:4

Thin Slicing in Dating

Sacrifices for you	*Husbands, love your wives, as Christ loved the church and gave himself up for her,... In the same way husbands should love their wives as their own bodies. He who loves his wife loves himself. For no one ever hated his own flesh, but nourishes and cherishes it, just as Christ does the church.* Ephesians 5:25, 28-29
Makes you the top priority	*"Therefore a man shall leave his father and mother and hold fast to his wife, and the two shall become one flesh." This mystery is profound, and I am saying that it refers to Christ and the church. However, let each one of you love his wife as himself, and let the wife see that she respects her husband.* Ephesians 5:31-33

Trustworthy	The heart of her husband trusts in her, and he will have no lack of gain. She does him good, and not harm, all the days of her life. Proverbs 31:11-12
Will take care of the family	She seeks wool and flax, and works with willing hands. She is like the ships of the merchant; she brings her food from afar. Proverbs 31:13-14
Willing to work to provide	She rises while it is yet night and provides food for her household and portions for her maidens. Proverbs 31:15
Compassionate	She opens her hand to the poor and reaches out her hands to the needy. Proverbs 31:20
Honorable	Her husband is known in the gates when he sits among the elders of the land. She makes linen garments and sells them; she delivers sashes to the merchant. Strength and dignity are her clothing, and she laughs at the time to come. Proverbs 31:23-25
Wise and Kind	She opens her mouth with wisdom, and the teaching of kindness is on her tongue. Proverbs 31:26

I experienced a bit of this kind of thin slicing when I was in college. We had a tradition where young men would send letters to young women each night and the women would reciprocate. Keep in mind this was well before the days of cell phones. So it was a big deal for all of us. People would wait around and look forward to the letters each evening. One night I was walking by the library and a young woman told me she bet she could get every girl from the girl's dorm to write me. It was a big joke and she tried to make it happen. Later that night it appeared, I had letters from everyone in the girl's dorm.

As I went through the letters, I noted there was at least one girl who did not send a letter—Lynne Harmon. She sent me a subtle message that night. If you want a letter from me, you'll need to write me first. I got the message. Several years later, she became my wife.

> Build houses and live in them; plant gardens and
> eat their produce. Take wives and have sons and
> daughters; take wives for your sons, and give your
> daughters in marriage, that they may bear sons and
> daughters; multiply there, and do not decrease. But
> seek the welfare of the city where I have sent you
> into exile, and pray to the Lord on its behalf, for in its
> welfare you will find your welfare.
> Jeremiah 29:5-7

Invest in the Culture

Jeremiah told the exiles to seek the welfare of the city where they were sent. You too must seek to help the community wherever you go. You are prepared. You know who you are and are part of a community of believers. Head into the corrupt culture as Daniel, Hananiah, Mishael, and Azariah did. Perhaps you are in a workplace where you are the only Christian, a secular university where many are antagonistic to your faith, or a missionary in a place where no one knows about Christ. You are in the culture. What do you do?

> Do all things without grumbling or disputing, that
> you may be blameless and innocent, children of
> God without blemish in the midst of a crooked and
> twisted generation, among whom you shine as lights
> in the world, holding fast to the word of life...
> Philippians 2:14-16a

Resist the Urge to Complain

Instead of grumbling consider the words of Mordecai to Esther (Esther 4:14) long ago when she found herself in a corrupt culture, "Who knows whether you have not come ... for such a time as this?" Embrace the admonition of Paul and seek to influence the culture without grumbling. We can have an influence by living blamelessly. It is easy to become bitter about what has happened to our culture but this can lead us to harm others rather than pointing them to God.

Look for Opportunities

Look for opportunities to be salt and light to those around you. Be patient, they will come, but when they do be ready to seize the moment. Consider how Daniel was ready when Nebuchadnezzar ordered the killing of the wise men. Instead of being consumed with his own concerns, he calmly sought a solution and saved the wise men.

A Crisis Leads to an Opportunity

The king answered and said to the Chaldeans "The word from me is firm: if you do not make known to me the dream and its interpretation you shall be torn limb from limb and your houses shall be laid in ruins."
Daniel 2:5

He declared to Arioch, the king's captain, "Why is the decree of the king so urgent?" Then Arioch made the matter known to Daniel. And Daniel went in and requested the king to appoint him a time, that he might show the interpretation to the king.
Daniel 2:15-16

Therefore Daniel went in to Arioch, whom the king had appointed to destroy the wise men of Babylon. He went and said thus to him: "Do not destroy the wise men of Babylon; bring me in before the king, and I will show the king the interpretation."
Daniel 2:24

Though his life was in danger, Daniel laid the groundwork by briefly mentioning God when he was brought before King Nebuchadnezzar.

Daniel answered the king and said, "No wise men, enchanters, magicians, or astrologers can show to the king the mystery that the king has asked, but there is a God in heaven who reveals mysteries, and he has made known to King Nebuchadnezzar what will be in the latter days. Your dream and the visions of your head as you lay in bed are these.
Daniel 2:27-28

At the conclusion of the interpretation of the dream, Daniel stated

"...just as you saw that a stone was cut from a mountain by no human hand, and that it broke in pieces the iron, the bronze, the clay, the silver, and the gold. A great God has made known to the king what shall be after this. The dream is certain, and its interpretation sure."
Daniel 2:45

When you receive an opportunity, be clear, concise, and congenial in your presentation of the gospel. Also, remember our Sovereign God will present other opportunities and use other people to influence the culture. Later God used Hananiah, Mishael, and Azariah to influence King Nebuchadnezzar during the fiery furnace incident where they briefly witnessed to him.

Shadrach, Meshach, and Abednego answered and said to the king, "O Nebuchadnezzar, we have no need to answer you in this matter. If this be so, our God whom we serve is able to deliver us from the burning fiery furnace, and he will deliver us out of your hand, O king. But if not, be it known to you, O king, that we will not serve your gods or worship the golden image that you have set up."
Daniel 3:16-18

Be prepared to present a witness on the Bible as the Word of God, the resurrection of Christ, God's plan for the family, and your own reason for hope. Look forward to these opportunities rather than avoiding them.

But in your hearts honor Christ the Lord as holy, always being prepared to make a defense to anyone who asks you for a reason for the hope that is in you; <u>yet do it with gentleness and respect</u>.
1 Peter 3:15

Modern Day Examples

We have two U.S. Army Chaplains that came out of the church where I pastor. Chaplain David Trogdon and Tracy Kerr both served in Afghanistan and Iraq.

> See Chaplain David Trogdon discuss ministering in Iraq and Afghanistan at survivingculture.com

After getting their bachelor degrees at Welch College they went on to Southeastern Baptist Theological Seminary

> Hear Cuban Physicist Miguel Benitez discuss character in a corrupt culture on the streets of Havana at survivingculture.com

and earned master of divinity degrees to qualify as chaplains. They also worked in our church with people struggling with a variety of difficulties. Since leaving our church they have both experieced multiple deployments to combat theaters and have dealt with the unthinkable on a daily basis. They have had to help soldiers who have had to take the lives of others. They have helped those who have been maimed in terrible ways and who have lost their buddies in the process. Chaplain Kerr helped soldiers who aided soldiers who had encountered a toddler that could barely walk that approached them wearing a suicide bomb vest resulting in horific consequences. Sometimes soldiers are just riding down the road and a bomb explodes taking the life of a buddy. At one time Chaplain Trogdon worked with a team that dismantles bombs, when they failed there were horific consequences. There are a lot of people who would love to help those soldiers but they cannot unless they have prepared. Chaplain Trogdon and Chaplain Kerr got into a position to serve. They developed qualities in their work in the local church that enabled them to help others. They also took the time to get the educational training required to be a U.S. military chaplain. Those qualities were not developed at the spur of the moment. They were prepared when the opportunities arose to influence their community.

Be a Small Target

In 1 Peter 4:15-16 the Scripture says, "But let none of you suffer as a murderer or a thief or an evildoer or as a meddler. Yet if anyone suffers as a Christian, let him not be ashamed, but let him glorify God in that name." In essence, Peter is telling us to be a small target. If we are going to get in trouble, let it be for doing what we should do, instead of what we should not do.

Try to be a person of integrity so that no one will have a reason to attack you. Hananiah, Mishael, and Azariah did not get into trouble because they were slack at their work. They were attacked because they refused to bow to Nebuchadnezzar's image (Daniel 3:8-12).

When it came time to try to attack Daniel there was nothing that could be used against him except his faith. Daniel 6:5 says, "Then these men said, 'We shall not find any ground for complaint against this Daniel unless we find it in connection with the law of his God.'" Let that be the case for you as well. And don't worry, God will take care of your enemies for you.

Enemies are Opportunities

Did Daniel have anything to be angry about?

Mistreatment of his king	Against him came up Nebuchadnezzar king of Babylon and bound him in chains to take him to Babylon. 2 Chronicles 36:6
Mistreatment of the weak	Therefore he brought up against them the king of the Chaldeans, who killed their young men with the sword in the house of their sanctuary and had no compassion on young man or virgin, old man or aged. He gave them all into his hand. 2 Chronicles 36:17
Destruction of the homeland	And they burned the house of God and broke down the wall of Jerusalem and burned all its palaces with fire and destroyed all its precious vessels. 2 Chronicles 36:19
Killing of a king's sons	Then they captured the king and brought him up to the king of Babylon at Riblah, and they passed sentence on him. They slaughtered the sons of Zedekiah before his eyes, and put out the eyes of Zedekiah and bound him in chains and took him to Babylon. 2 Kings 25:6-7
Attempted to kill his friends	Then Nebuchadnezzar was filled with fury, and the expression of his face was changed against Shadrach, Meshach, and Abednego. He ordered the furnace heated seven times more than it was usually heated. And he ordered some of the mighty men of his army to bind Shadrach, Meshach, and Abednego, and to cast them into the burning fiery furnace. Daniel 3:19-20

Before Jesus instructed us in Matthew 5:44 to "love your enemies and pray for those who persecute you" Daniel put that into practice. Nebuchadnezzar encountered many obstacles as we will see later. Each time, it appears Daniel did his best to help him. If you had been in Daniel's shoes would you have been willing to help Nebuchadnezzar? Consider the previous chart which shows the many reasons Daniel could have been angry with Nebuchadnezzar.

For 18 years, Judah was oppressed by the Babylonian regime. This oppression culminated with the destruction of Jerusalem and the burning of the temple in 586 B.C. If you were doing a modern day Hollywood movie about the lives of Daniel, Hananiah, Mishael, and Azariah it would probably involve them seeking revenge for what was done to their homeland.

Daniel clearly had a reason to be angry with Nebuchadnezzar. However, I believe as Dr. Douglas Simpson suggested in his book on Daniel that he prayed for Nebuchadnezzar for some 30 years. Perhaps Daniel's approach began, as Jesus would later command with praying for an enemy.

> *Then Daniel, whose name was Belteshazzar, was dismayed for a while, and his thoughts alarmed him. The king answered and said, "Belteshazzar, let not the dream or the interpretation alarm you." Belteshazzar answered and said, "My lord, may the dream be for those who hate you and its interpretation for your enemies!"*
> *Daniel 4:19*

When we care for an enemy as Jesus commanded, it truly sets the believer apart from the non-believer. How do we know that Daniel was not filled with hatred toward Nebuchadnezzar? In Daniel 4:19-27, we see Daniel relay the news to Nebuchadnezzar that he would lose his mind. This was the perfect time for Daniel to gloat in the misfortune of this man who had done so much harm to those he loved. Yet Daniel did not gloat. He was dismayed when he realized the trouble that is about to befall the king. Daniel tried to help Nebuchadnezzar.

> Therefore, O king, let my counsel be acceptable to you: break off your sins by practicing righteousness, and your iniquities by showing mercy to the oppressed, that there may perhaps be a lengthening of your prosperity."
> Daniel 4:27

He truly cared about Nebuchadnezzar. You must have the same concern for those in your community.

Forgive

Some might say that Daniel had over identified with his captor and that he had tried to suppress what Nebuchadnezzar had truly done to him and Judah. I suggest instead that Daniel had truly forgiven Nebuchadnezzar. I also suspect we can learn from him as well. It is critical that we forgive if we are to have physical, spiritual, and psychological health.

Jesus' Solution for Enemies

"You have heard that it was said, 'You shall love your neighbor and hate your enemy.' But I say to you, Love your enemies and pray for those who persecute you, so that you may be sons of your Father who is in heaven. For he makes his sun rise on the evil and on the good, and sends rain on the just and on the unjust. For if you love those who love you, what reward do you have? Do not even the tax collectors do the same?
Matthew 5:43-46

Pray for the Offender

In studies on forgiveness, those in prayer and devotional groups have been found to be more likely to forgive. It appears that when we pray for an offender, we develop empathy for them. Similarly, when we read biblical passages on forgiveness we are more likely to forgive.[64]

In his work on forgiveness, Dr. Robert Enright indicated there is a process many appear to go through as they forgive. This includes an acknowledgement of what has been done, gaining perspective upon what has happened, and building positive thoughts and behaviors.[65] Nearly 70 years after the exile began, Daniel prayed about what had happened to Judah. He made it clear that it was a calamity.

Acknowledgement of a Calamity

By bringing upon us a great calamity. For under the whole heaven there has not been done anything like what has been done against Jerusalem.
Daniel 9:12b

As it is written in the Law of Moses, all this calamity has come upon us; yet we have not entreated the favor of the LORD our God, turning from our iniquities and gaining insight by your truth. Daniel 9:13

Therefore the Lord has kept ready the calamity and has brought it upon us, for the Lord our God is righteous in all the works that he has done, and we have not obeyed his voice. Daniel 9:14

However, Daniel also acknowledged that Judah had behaved treacherously thereby providing some perspective for what had transpired. We can learn from him by acknowledging when we have been wronged and searching for perspective upon what has happened.

Too often we assume that when we have been wronged our life has been irreparably damaged and even shortened. That was not the case with Daniel or apparently with other people. For example, an interesting study out of the University of Haifa in Israel examined 55,000 Polish immigrants who came to Israel between 1945 until

1950 and another group that came prior to 1939. The researchers found that the men who had experienced the Holocaust at 10 to 15 years of age lived on average 10 months more than the men who were already in Israel. Youth who were 16 to 20 years of age and experienced the Holocaust lived an extra 18 months longer than those who did not experience the Holocaust. It has been hypothesized that the Holocaust survivors lived longer in spite of the trauma they experienced, because of a renewed sense of purpose and meaning.[66]

From the Scripture it appears that Daniel understood that Nebuchadnezzar's actions were brought on by the sins of Judah. This probably prevented him from sitting around and thinking about how evil Nebuchadnezzar was and allowed him to move forward and minister to Nebuchadnezzar. Similarly, Joseph acknowledged the evil his brothers perpetrated upon him in Genesis 50. Yet, he appeared to have a perspective for the situation and indicated the event had been used by God to save many people. The lesson for us is not to minimize some evil someone has done to us, but to acknowledge it and try to move past it, looking for perspective, how something positive might come out of it and then to move on.

Also, it is not wise to simply dwell on how we have been wronged or a person with whom we have had a difficulty. For example, the research indicates that using Facebook to keep tabs on an ex after a breakup may delay emotional recovery and personal growth. In one study, people who spent the most time on their ex-partner's Facebook page had more distress, negative feelings, and longing for their former flames and lower levels of personal growth.[67] As Proverbs 26:20 says, "For lack of wood the fire goes out, and where there is no whisperer, quarreling ceases."

If your enemy is hungry, give him bread to eat, and if
he is thirsty, give him water to drink.
Proverbs 25:21

Do something good for your enemy

It appears that as a young man Daniel is trying to point Nebuchadnezzar to God when the lives of the wise men were threatened. Before interpreting Nebuchadnezzar's dream, Daniel said, "There is a God in heaven who reveals mysteries, and he has made known to King Nebuchadnezzar what will be in the latter days. Your dream and the visions of your head as you lay in bed are these" (Daniel 2:28). Daniel was witnessing to Nebuchadnezzar, trying to show him the truth.

We can learn from Daniel, when we do something nice for someone it makes us have a more positive view of them. When we harm someone or talk despairingly about them, it leads us to dislike them more. Part of the forgiveness process for Daniel was actually trying to help Nebuchadnezzar find God.

Was it worth it?

It appears Nebuchadnezzar became quite fond of Daniel. When Daniel interpreted Nebuchadnezzar's dream, according to Daniel 2:46, "King Nebuchadnezzar fell upon his face and paid homage to Daniel, and commanded that an offering and incense be offered up to him." Nebuchadnezzar also began to speak favorably of God, "The king answered and said to Daniel, "Truly, your God is God of gods and Lord of kings, and a revealer of mysteries, for you have been able to reveal this mystery." Though Nebuchadnezzar did not immediately become a follower of God, he acknowledged God's supremacy as a god, and kept Daniel close throughout his reign (Daniel 2:49).

Critics often look at Daniel 3 and ask about the whereabouts of Daniel during the fiery furnace episode. As you interact with people in the culture you will learn that people who have authority over you might not want you around when they are about to make a decision about which they know you will disagree. Nebuchadnezzar would have known Daniel well enough to realize he would object to the building of his golden image, and would never bow to such a thing. I also suspect he was fond enough of Daniel (or dependent upon his expertise) that he did not wish to lose him. To deal with this I think Nebuchadnezzar would have sent Daniel away on business during this time. If this is what transpired it shows that Nebuchadnezzar did not want Daniel around when he did something he ought not to do and it suggests that Daniel was having an impact upon his culture.

In Daniel 2 Nebuchadnezzar praises God but then falters with the building of the fiery furnace in Daniel 3. The next interaction we see between Nebuchadnezzar and Daniel is in Daniel 4. It is important to note that Nebuchadnezzar is doing the talking in this example. Note the similarity between Daniel 4:3 and Psalm 145:13.

How great are his signs, how mighty his wonders!
His kingdom is an everlasting kingdom, and his do-
minion endures from generation to generation.
Daniel 4:3

Your kingdom is an everlasting kingdom, and your
dominion endures throughout all generations.
Psalm 145:13

After King Nebuchadnezzar recounts his experience, he appears to acknowledge God as the God.

At the end of the days I, Nebuchadnezzar, lifted my
eyes to heaven, and my reason returned to me, and
I blessed the Most High, and praised and honored
him who lives forever, for his dominion is an everlast-
ing dominion, and his kingdom endures from gen-

> *eration to generation; all the inhabitants of the earth*
> *are accounted as nothing, and he does according*
> *to his will among the host of heaven and among*
> *the inhabitants of the earth; and none can stay his*
> *hand or say to him, "What have you done?...Now*
> *I, Nebuchadnezzar, praise and extol and honor the*
> *King of heaven, for all his works are right and his*
> *ways are just; and those who walk in pride he is able*
> *to humble.*
> Daniel 4:34-35, 37

Did Nebuchadnezzar become a believer? I do not know, but one thing is certain. He was definitely influenced by some exiles from Judah.

Don't Quit!

Still at Work

Belshazzar did not appear to have a high regard for Daniel. That did not stop Daniel from faithfully working. It was during Belshazzar's reign that we received those interesting visions.

In the first year of Belshazzar king of Babylon, Daniel saw a dream and visions of his head as he lay in his bed. Then he wrote down the dream and told the sum of the matter.
Daniel 7:1

In the third year of the reign of King Belshazzar a vision appeared to me, Daniel, after that which appeared to me at the first.
Daniel 8:1

It appears that the descendants of Nebuchadnezzar did not value Daniel. But when Belshazzar needed some help with an interpretation, the Queen Mother reminded him of a man "in whom is the spirit of the holy gods." She lists specific character qualities Daniel possessed. Belshazzar sent for Daniel and seems to treat him with disrespect by calling him an exile. This shows you that though you may not be valued, if you possess competence people will eventually seek out your services.

Daniel was competent enough to serve in whatever administration might be in power. He served at least until 539 B.C. In Daniel 6, a new administration arose and the king saw Daniel's competence and made him one of three governors (Daniel 6:2). Look at verse 3.

Then this Daniel became distinguished above all the other high officials and satraps, because an excellent spirit was in him. And the king planned to set him over the whole kingdom.
Daniel 6:3

Daniel was likable and that attitude distinguished him. Daniel could do things that needed done. To the point that his enemies could only find one fault in him—he prayed. They attacked his identity as a follower of God. A law was passed making it illegal to pray. Seventy years later Daniel faces another test. How did he respond?

When Daniel knew that the document had been signed, he went to his house where he had windows in his upper chamber open toward Jerusalem. He got down on his knees three times a day and prayed and gave thanks before his God, as he had done previously.
Daniel 6:10

Daniel prayed in obedience to 2 Chronicles 6:38-39 by praying toward Jerusalem. He would rather die than change the way he prayed. When the king learned Daniel had violated the decree, he was angry with himself (Daniel 6:14). He began searching for a way to save Daniel but he could not (Daniel 6:15). As you read the passage it appears that the king is more frightened for Daniel than Daniel may have been (Daniel 6:16-18).

> *As he came near to the den where Daniel was, he cried out in a tone of anguish. The king declared to Daniel, "O Daniel, servant of the living God, has your God, whom you serve continually, been able to deliver you from the lions?" Then Daniel said to the king, "O king, live forever! My God sent his angel and shut the lions' mouths, and they have not harmed me, because I was found blameless before him; and also before you, O king, I have done no harm." Then the king was exceedingly glad, and commanded that Daniel be taken up out of the den. So Daniel was taken up out of the den, and no kind of harm was found on him, because he had trusted in his God.*
> *Daniel 6:20-23*

After the sleepless night, the king ran to the lion's den. Notice he didn't say, "Belteshazzar, has your God saved you?" Daniel, whose name means "God is judge," says in verse 22 "I was found blameless." Daniel won the moment he got on his knees and prayed toward Jerusalem. Wow, what a story. Could God use you like that? But that was Daniel, real people in the 21st century don't act that way.

> **Where is Daniel Buried?**
>
> Would you like to visit the grave of Daniel? You can visit a Tomb of Daniel in Susa, Iran. However, near Mala Amir, in Khuzestan of Iran there are others who claim to have the grave of Daniel. There are tombs for Daniel in Iraq as well (Babylon, Kirkuk, and Muqdadiyah). There is at least one more site that claims to have the tomb of Daniel, that is found in Samarkand, Uzbekistan. Not bad for a fellow who was an exile.

A Life Well Lived

Perhaps you have heard of Al Braca who lived in Leonardo, N.J. with his wife, Jean. He was a regular guy, with four children. His daughter became ill and in the process of that illness, Al and Jean met the Lord. He claimed that the Lord healed his daughter of a rare blood disease. Al was a deacon and in charge of discipling new believers at his church. Al's job was hard. Not doing the job—Al excelled at that, but the culture where he worked was often hostile toward him. They picked on Al, called him "the Rev," and put filthy screen savers on his computer. Al hated his job and thought of leaving. Finally, he decided that God wanted him to stay, and be blameless and harmless in the midst of a corrupt culture. So that's what Al did.

He noticed that the people began to bring their problems to him. Al was someone they could confide and he would pray with them. There was a fire at his company, he helped someone out who had asthma, and people remembered that.

Then on September 11, 2001, Al was at work on the 110th floor of World Trade Center Building 1 in the office of Cantor Fitzgerald. Cantor Fitzgerald had over 700 employees at work that day. None survived. After the first plane hit at 8:45 am, several Cantor Fitzgerald employees called their loved ones and said their goodbyes. Many of the employees told their families they were okay, they had prayed with Al. Al had prayed for these people regularly for years without much success. Apparently, many of them prayed with him in their last moments. Many calls and emails indicate that Al led a prayer meeting and shared Christ with more than 50 people in a big circle that day.[68]

At 10:29 am, World Trade Center Building 1 collapsed. That was 104 minutes after the plane hit it. That is not a lot of time. There was no time to prepare to share the Lord. There was no time to get educated or for Al to become what he needed to be spiritually. One hundred and four minutes is not a lot of time—unless one has spent decades being what God made them to be—in that case 104 minutes is all that is needed.

Al had been preparing for those 104 minutes all of his Christian life. Thank God, Al Braca had prepared and persevered. Many of those who mocked and made fun of him in earlier years might have prayed with him in those final moments.

What about you? Are you prepared to go beyond surviving and shine in a crooked culture? Will you be prepared to serve tomorrow? The God who is preparing you today knows what is around the corner tomorrow.

What will happen to the people you interact with in the days and years ahead? Do not just mark time. Get prepared to serve and be a person of substance. Influence the culture rather than allowing it to affect you. The fate of those people will largely be determined by how you spend your time today. It is up to you.

notes

1 Pew Research Center (2010). Religion Among Milennials: http://www.pewforum. org/2010/02/17/religion-among-the-millennials/.

2 E. J. Young (1977). The Prophecy of Daniel. Grand Rapids, MI: Eerdmans Publishing.

3 D. Ariely (2012). The (Honest) Truth About Dishonesty. New York, NY: Harper Collins.

4 J. G. Baldwin (1978). Daniel: Tyndale Old Testament Commentaries. Downers Gove, IL: Intervarsity Press.

5 E. J. Young (1977). Ibid.

6 R. Cialdini (1984). Influence: The Psychology of Persuasion. New York, NY: Harper Collins.

7 J. J. Arnett, J. J. (2000). Emerging adulthood: A theory of development from the late teens through the twenties. American Psychologist, 55(5), 469–480. doi:10.1037/0003-066X.55.5.469.

R. D. Stinson (2010). Hooking up in young adulthood: A review of factors influencing the sexual behavior of college students. Journal of College Student Psychotherapy, 24(2), 98–115. doi:10.1080/87568220903558596.

8 C. M. Grello, D. P. Welsh, M. S. Harper, & J. W. Dickson (2003). Dating and sexual relationship trajectories and adolescent functioning. Adolescent & Family Health, 3(3), 103–112.

9 M. L. Fisher, K. Worth, J. R. Garcia, & T. Meredith (2012). Feelings of regret following uncommitted sexual encounters in Canadian university students. Culture, Health & Sexuality, 14(1), 45–57. doi:10.1080/13691058.2011.619579.

W. F. Flack Jr., K. A. Daubman, M. L. Caron, J. A. Asadorian, N. R. D'Aureli, S. N. Gigliotti, ...E. R. Stine (2007). Risk factors and consequences of unwanted sex among university students: Hooking up, alcohol, and stress response. Journal of Interpersonal Violence, 22(2), 139–157. doi:10.1177/0886260506295354

A. Miller (2013). New insights on college drinking: Psychologists' research is pinpointing who is most at risk for drinking problems in college and developing more targeted, evidence-based interventions. Monitor on Psychology, 44(9), 46-51.

[10] L. D. Johnston, P. M. O'Malley, & J. G. Bachman (2003). Monitoring the Future National Survey Results on Drug Use, 1975–2002: Vol. II. College Students and Young Adults Ages 19–40. (NIH Pub. No. 03–5376). Bethesda, MD: National Institute of Drug Abuse, 2003.

[11] M. Windle. Alcohol use among adolescents and young adults. National Institute of Alcohol Abuse and Alcoholism. Accessed at http://pubs.niaaa.nih.gov/publications/arh27-1/79-86.htm on December 23, 2013.

[12] D. T. Neal, W. Wood, & A. Drolet (2013). How do people adhere to goals when willpower is low? The profits (and pitfalls) of strong habits. Journal of Personality and Social Psychology, 104(6), 959-975. doi:10.1037/a0032626.

[13] T. Longman (1999). Daniel: The NIV Application Commentary. Grand Rapids, MI: Zondervan Publishing.

[14] M. Gladwell (2008). Outliers: The Story of Success. New York, NY: Little, Brown & Company.

[15] K. Weir (2013). Never a dull moment. Monitor on Psychology, 44(7) 54-57.

[16] H. Gardner (2011). Frames of Mind: The Theory of Multiple Intelligences. New York, NY: Basic Books.

[17] L. Hao & H. S. Woo (2012). Distinct Trajectories in the Transition to Adulthood: Are Children of Immigrants Advantaged? Child Development, 83(5), 1623-39. doi:10.1111/j.1467-8624.2012.01798.x.

[18] L. Winerman (December, 2013). Questionnaire: What sets high achievers apart? Interview with Angela Lee Duckworth. Monitor on Psychology, 44(11), 28-31.

[19] M. Gladwell (2008). Ibid.

[20] R. Murray (November 21, 2012). Woman on unpaid leave after taking disrespectful photo next to soldier's grave during work trip. New York Daily News. http://www.nydailynews.com/news/national/vulgar-facebook-pic-woman-canned-article-1.1205609#ixzz2nE7eQjlw. Accessed on November 12, 2013.

[21] C. Pearson, L. M. Andersson, & C. L. Porath (2005). Workplace Incivility. In Counterproductive Work Behavior (Ed. S. Fox & P. E. Spector) pages 177-200. Washington, D.C.: American Psychological Association.

[22] M. Gladwell (2005). Blink: The Power of Thinking without Thinking. New York, NY: Little, Brown & Company.

[23] D. Goleman (1994). Emotional Intelligence. New York, NY: Bantam Books.

[24] M. Csikszentmihalyi (1997). Creativity. New York, NY: Harper Collins.

[25] M. Csikszentmihalyi (1990). Flow. New York, NY: Harper Collins.

[26] L. G. Knapp, J. E. Kelly-Reid, & S. A. Ginder (2012). Enrollment in Postsecondary Institutions, Fall 2011; Financial Statistics, Fiscal Year 2011; and Graduation Rates, Selected Cohorts, 2003-2008. Washington, DC: U.S. Department of Education. http://nces.ed.gov/pubs2012/2012174rev.pdf)

[27] Strong Interest Inventory Resource Strategies for Group and Individual Interpretations in College Settings (1995).

[28] Strong (1995). Ibid.

29 Strong (1995). Ibid.

30 Strong (1995). Ibid.

31 Strong (1995). Ibid.

32 Strong (1995). Ibid.

33 I. B. Myers, & P. B. Myers (1980). Gifts Differing: Understanding Personality Type. Palo Alto, CA: Davies-Black Publishing, Inc.

34 D. Hembrick (2012). Eagle Career Network. Durham, NC: North Carolina Central University.

35 The Federal Trade Commission. Choosing a Vocational School. Accessed at http://www.consumer.ftc.gov/articles/0241-choosing-vocational-school on December 26, 2013.

36 N. J. Roese, & A. Summerville (2005). What we regret most…and why. Personality and Social Psychology Bulletin, 31(9), 1273-1285. doi:10.1177/0146167205274693.

37 L. G. Knapp, et al. (2012). Ibid.

38 D. J. Foss (2013). Your complete guide to college success: How to study smart, achieve your goals, and enjoy campus life. Washington, DC: American Psychological Association.

39 D. J. Foss (2013). Ibid.

40 D. J. Foss (2013). Ibid.

41 D. J. Foss (2013). Ibid.

42 D. J. Foss (2013). Ibid.

43 D. J. Foss (2013). Ibid.

44 J. L. Walsh, R. Fielder, K. B. Carey, & M. P. Carey (March 26, 2013). Female College Students' Media Use and Academic Outcomes: Results from a Longitudinal Cohort. Emerging Adulthood, from http://eax.sagepub.com/content/early/2013/03/05/2167696813479780.

45 D. J. Foss (2013). Ibid.

46 D. J. Foss (2013). Ibid.

47 D. J. Foss (2013). Ibid.

48 D. Hembrick (2012). Ibid.

49 Autin, F. & Croizet, J.C. (2012). Improving working memory efficiency by reframing metacognitive interpretation of task difficulty. Journal of Experimental Psychology: General, 141(4), 610-618.

50 T. D. Wilson (2012). Redirect: The Surprising New Science of Psychological Change. New York, NY: Penguin Group.

51 R. Pastore (2012). 6 Strategies for successful schmoozing. Monitor on Psychology, 43(7), 80-82.

52 E. B. Yost, & M. A. Corbishley (1987). Career Counseling: A Psychological Approach. San Francisco, CA: Jossey-Bass, Inc.

[53] Gallup. State of the American Workplace Report 2013: Employee Engagement Insights for U.S. Business Leaders. Assessed at http://www.gallup.com/strategicconsulting/163007/state-american-workplace.aspx on December 30, 2013. Washington, DC:Gallup.

[54] M. McPherson, L. Smith-Loving, & M. E. Brashers (2006). Social isolation in America: Changes in core discussion networks over two decades. American Sociological Review, 71(3), 353-375.

[55] D. Blansky, C. Kavanaugh, C. Boothroyd, B. Benson, J. Gallagher, John Endress, Hiroki Sayama (2013). Spread of Academic Success in a High School Social Network. PLoS ONE, 8(2): e55944 doi:10.1371/journal.pone.0055944.

[56] S. Burd-Sharps, & K. Lewis (2012). One in Seven. Brooklyn, New York: Measure of America. Accessed at http://www.measureofamerica.org/wp-content/uploads/2012/09/MOA-One_in_Seven09-14.pdf on December 30, 2013.

[57] M. Gladwell (2005). Ibid.

[58] A. Miller (2013). The Science of karma: Organizational psychologist and top-rated Wharton professor Adam Grant says one secret to success is helping others succeed. Monitor on Psychology, 44(9), 28.

[59] M. McPherson, et al. (2006). Ibid.

[60] M. E. Brashears (2011). "Small networks and high isolation?: A reexamination of American discussion networks." Social Networks. 33(4): 331-341.

[61] A. K. Przybylski, & N. Weinstein (2013). Can you connect with me now? How the presence of mobile communication technology influences face-to-face conversation quality. Journal of Social and Personal Relationships, 30(3), 237-246.

[62] D. Cohn, J. S. Passel, W. Wang, & G. Livingston (December 14, 2011). Barely Half of U.S. Adults Are Married – A Record Low. Pew Research Social Demographics and Change. Washington, D.C.: Pew Research Center. Assessed at http://www.pewsocialtrends.org/2011/12/14/barely-half-of-u-s-adults-are-married-a-record-low/ on December 31, 2013.

[63] J. Gottman (1995). Why Marriages Succeed or Fail. New York, NY: Fireside.

[64] S. L. Vasiliauskas, & M. R. McMinn (2012). The Effects of a Prayer Intervention on the Process of Forgiveness. Psychology of Religion and Spirituality, 5(1), 23-32.

[65] R. D. Enright (2001). Forgiveness is a Choice. Washington, D.C: American Psychological Association.

[66] A. Sagi-Schwartz, M. J. Bakermans-Kranenburg, S. Linn S, & M. H. van IJzendoorn (2013). Against All Odds: Genocidal Trauma Is Associated with Longer Life-Expectancy of the Survivors. PLoS ONE 8(7): e69179. doi:10.1371/journal.pone.0069179.

[67] C. Tara Marshall (2012). Cyberpsychology, Behavior, and Social Networking, 15(10): 521-526. doi:10.1089/cyber.2012.0125.

[68] C. Ditchfield (2002). A Light in the Darkness. Colorado Springs, CO: Focus on the Family Magazine.